Leading
for Equity

The Pursuit of Excellence in Montgomery County Public Schools

STACEY M. CHILDRESS

DENIS P. DOYLE

DAVID A. THOMAS

HARVARD EDUCATION PRESS
CAMBRIDGE, MASSACHUSETTS

Sixth Printing, 2016

Library of Congress Control Number 2009925548
Paperback ISBN 978-1-934742-22-8
Library Edition ISBN 978-1-934742-23-5

Published by Harvard Education Press,
an imprint of the Harvard Education Publishing Group
Harvard Education Press
8 Story Street
Cambridge, MA 02138

Cover design: Perry Lubin

Contents

Foreword by David Gergen   v

Introduction   1

1   Challenging the Status Quo   13

2   Implementing a Differentiation Strategy   33

3   Building Relationships for Sustainability   55

4   Expanding Capacity Through Investments in People   73

5   Designing New Systems and Structures for Change   93

6   Creating an Equity-Focused Culture   111

7   Six Lessons from the Montgomery County Journey   131
     and a New Call to Action

8   Strategy as Problem Solving—Applying the   149
     MCPS Approach

     Notes   171

     Acknowledgments   175

     About the Authors   177

     Index   179

Foreword

by David Gergen

Leading for Equity

A quarter century ago, a national blue-ribbon commission on public education warned that a "rising tide of mediocrity" was sweeping across our schools and that, unless reversed, it would do more harm to the country than any outside enemy could inflict. That report in the early 1980s touched off a reform movement in public education that in recent years has grown ever more powerful. Now, with an Obama administration coming to Washington, hopes for dramatic change are perhaps at their zenith.

If it comes, it will not be a moment too soon. Most educators believe that in recent decades we have indeed made progress in improving the quality of public education, but that progress has been slow, often halting, and is not keeping up with the rising demands of the twenty-first century workplace. We talk blithely of leaving no child behind; in truth, we are leaving behind millions upon millions. We are kidding ourselves in not calling it a national scandal. In the short term, we are preoccupied with rebuilding our economy, but in the long term, reform of public education may be the single most important challenge facing America.

By the year 2050—just over forty years from now—whites will compose less than half the population of the country. In most major urban systems, minorities are already well over half of all students. Yet the starkest differences in educational opportunity and achievement are those between African American, Hispanic, and other minority children, especially in low-income areas, and their more affluent counterparts. By the time they are in the third or fourth grades, low-income minority students are on average nearly three grade levels behind in reading and math. The vast majority never catch up. At best, only half graduate from high school, and in our urban areas, graduation rates for low-income and minority students are closer to 30 percent. These disparities continue through college, so that only a small fraction wind up with a college degree. By the time they are in their twenties, their life pattern has been set—and it isn't pretty. The relentless pressures of globalization and technological change leave them unable to find jobs that pay well; college graduates earn twice as much as high school graduates, and the gap is increasing. For too many, early adulthood is a time of frustration, broken dreams, broken families, and living on the fringes of American life. Part of our economic distress today comes because we are on the front edge of a massive change in the workplace, one that as a matter of social justice as well as American competitiveness demands that we create a country where every child leaves school ready for college or a twenty-first-century job.

Yet the question arises, with the need for education reform so obvious and change so much in the air, what should we do? What will actually work? We have been wrestling with that question a good many years now, and while we have not reached a national consensus, the good news is that we do know some things that we did not know for sure a quarter century ago. Most importantly, we know that every child—regardless of income, family structure, or racial and ethnic background—is capable of learning if well taught. Anyone who has visited the Harlem Village Academies or a KIPP school in the South Bronx, or spent time with Teach For America, or been with a regular topflight schoolteacher has seen that firsthand. We know as well that individual schools are capable of turning around when they are led by caring, passionate principals and teachers. We know, too, that standards and accountability matter: if we set high standards and have an excellent school, student performance improves for students of low as well as high income. The blame for the state of our schools is not with our kids; it is with us, the adults, for not providing better teaching and public school leadership. So, we know some important things.

What we do not yet know for sure is whether we can move beyond improving the quality of a cluster of schools within a school district to achieving high performance across an entire district. Dedicated reformers and social entrepreneurs have opened the door to reform in a relatively small number of schools, but can we take reform to scale?

After all, our traditional public school districts still educate more than 85 percent of the nation's children.

The current discourse about large, urbanized school districts is usually that they are bloated, dysfunctional bureaucracies, full of entrenched employees who care more about their own interests than those of their students, and are therefore impossible to reform. This argument suggests that if we just legislate them out of existence and hand over the students to entrepreneurs, our problem would be solved. Perhaps, but the entrepreneurs would be the first to say this is unrealistic and that what is needed is to root a commitment to revolutionary reform within the school districts we have. That is exactly what is now starting to happen within a select number of large urban districts across the country where visionary and courageous reforms are at work, trying to change old patterns so that performance is no longer predictable by race and income. The best-known battlegrounds are in New York City, Washington, D.C., Chicago, Denver, Atlanta, and, increasingly, New Orleans; the struggles are not yet won, but they are in full swing. President Obama chose one of those reformers, former Chicago superintendent Arne Duncan, to serve as his secretary of education.

The authors of this invaluable book have chosen to focus on a lesser-known battleground but one that, because of its nature, is perhaps more broadly relevant to much of the nation. Certainly, the experiment with reform that is under way in the Montgomery County Public Schools in Maryland is rich in insights for reformers everywhere. The district is fascinating because its one hundred and forty thousand students represent basically two systems within one. Half of the county is largely white and affluent, and schools in these neighborhoods have long been some of the best in the nation. The other half consists of low-income and minority families, along with recent immigrants. A decade ago, schools in this part of Montgomery County looked similar to those in urban centers around the country—low performance levels that could be predicted with a high degree of certainty based on the racial and socioeconomic mix of the student population. In *Leading for Equity*, the authors, Childress, Doyle, and Thomas, tell the story of a ten-year journey from a status quo to a new order designed to achieve equitable access to achievement for every student, regardless of race or family income. Students from both lower- and higher-income families are much better off today than ten years ago.

There is not yet a fairy-tale ending in Montgomery County. The district has had setbacks along the way and still has mountains to climb. Nor is this a mythic account of a lone, heroic leader battling everyone else, especially teachers unions, in the service of children. Still, the journey has been remarkably successful so far—broad-based leadership from many individuals and groups, what they did, and why they did it. In the end, the Montgomery County journey shows what is possible when a visionary leader, thousands of committed educators (including teachers in unions), an elected school board, and students and their families work hard together toward achieving a common goal, even if they do not always agree on how to reach it.

Leading for Equity not only provides an enlightening account of progress in one school district; it also makes the lessons from Montgomery County relevant for others, proposing practical applications for education reformers of all stripes. At the end of chapter 7, the authors issue a call to action that is grounded in their research in Montgomery County but is aimed at the larger national conversation about transforming public education. Because they contain a classic American blend of hope and pragmatism, their insights and ideas are a welcome addition to the cause for reform. The years ahead are crucial for public education. I am among those who believe that evolution is no longer enough; only a revolution in American public education will meet the demands of social justice and twenty-first-century competition. Reading this book instills confidence that we can indeed make the leap from reforming a cluster of schools within a school district to reforming the district itself. That is cheering news at a time when the country needs a strong dose of optimism.

David Gergen
Director, Center for Public Leadership
Professor of public service
Harvard Kennedy School
January 2009

Introduction

In less than a decade, the Montgomery County Public Schools (MCPS) have been transformed into a system that is committed to providing all students, regardless of their race or family income, with access to an education that will prepare them for college and beyond. *Leading for Equity* tells this compelling American story: how the country's sixteenth-largest school district is tackling the achievement and opportunity challenges that confront the nation as a whole.

The journey begins with a visionary superintendent, but it does not end there. Broad-based leadership emerged from every quarter, including the school board and union officials, district and school staff, and elected county officials, all of whom had the courage to address issues of race and equity in the schools head-on. Together, they set out to break the link between race and class and academic outcomes. Their goal? High performance for all children in the district through accountability for the superintendent, board, teachers, and principals, along with the development of an organization that could sustain performance improvements over the long term. As we shall see, it is a journey without end. But while there is no finish line and still much work to do, there is measurable success.

MCPS serves about one hundred and forty thousand students in Maryland, adjacent to Washington, D.C. Every student subgroup has made significant gains since 1999—all races and ethnicities, all income levels, and those at the top and bottom of the performance curve. The highest performers continued to rise, while those at the lowest levels accelerated even faster, resulting in a narrowing of long-standing achievement gaps. All of this has happened while demographic changes have continued apace—during the time span of our story, the number of low-income students in the district rose nearly 6 points overall and even more in the areas of the county with the highest concentrations of poverty. *Leading for Equity* will explore this story in detail, but a few facts stand out:

- In 2002, only 59 percent of all kindergartners were able to read a simple story by the end of the year, including only 52 percent of African Americans and 42 percent of Hispanics. In 2008, 93 percent of students met an even more aggressive reading benchmark, with 91 percent of African Americans and 86 percent of Hispanics leaving kindergarten as readers. MCPS has raised the reading benchmark for 2009 to further increase the skills kindergartners will bring to first grade.

- In 2003, the gap between white and African American third graders on the Maryland state reading exam was 35 percentage points. By 2008, it had shrunk to 19 points. For Hispanics, the gap narrowed from 43 to 17 points. The trends in mathematics are similar.

- In 1999, 36 percent of all students enrolled in algebra by eighth grade, including 17 percent of African American students and 14 percent of Hispanic students. In 2008, 60 percent of all students, including 38 percent of African American and 39 percent of Hispanic students, enrolled in algebra by eighth grade. The district's goal is 80 percent in all student groups by 2014.

- In 1999, 54 percent of all high school students took at least one honors or advanced placement (AP) course, including 34 percent of African American and Hispanic students. In 2008, 74 percent of all students, including 59 percent of African Americans and 56 percent of Hispanics, enrolled in at least one honors or AP course. By 2014, the district's goal is 75 percent enrollment in all student groups.

Improvements of this magnitude in a district of this size in so little time are rare in public education. How is it that Montgomery County has been able to accelerate performance for those students who are farthest behind while continuing to raise the bar for everyone?

TWIN IMPERATIVES

MCPS is on a powerful journey that can inspire leaders, parents, and children around the country and could serve as one blueprint for reform in American education. At its base, it is a simple story driven by two imperatives—one moral, one economic.

First, the MCPS story embodies the moral imperative expressed over a century ago by educator John Dewey: *what the best and wisest parent wants for his own child, that must the community want for all its children.*[1] Indeed, whose child deserves to be left behind? At the dawn of a new millennium, race, ethnicity, and family income are highly correlated with academic outcomes in the United States. If you know a child's skin color and zip code, you can predict many things about her future. For instance, if she is from a high-poverty neighborhood, she is seven times less likely to graduate from college than an affluent student. If she is Hispanic, she is part of group that is, on average, three grade levels behind by age nine. In 2008, Americans took a huge step forward and elected the country's first black president, a man with a compelling life story that includes attendance at some of the best schools and universities the nation has to offer. His story should not be so unique. Every child should have access to the same high-quality education that President Barack Obama enjoyed. When that happens, race and class will cease to become so tightly linked with achievement and opportunity.

Second is the economic imperative: in the twenty-first-century economy, *human capital*—the economist's term of art for acquired knowledge, talent, skills, and dispositions—is the true source of wealth. As the world has moved away from locally based economies to an economy that is increasingly integrated and global, as technology solutions have helped us work smarter, our system of public education has resisted meaningful change for four generations. The future of our workforce, and indeed our country, is at stake. As the world grows more complex, the need for the next generation to be prepared to deal with the demands of new economic realities increases, and school systems must adapt and change their practices to produce lifelong learners equipped to handle the realities of an ever-changing world. No longer can we engage in old assumptions that led to the creation of a tiered system that sorts students based on the belief that only some children can learn at high levels.

Driven by these twin imperatives, Montgomery County Public Schools are rising to the occasion. In nine short years, MCPS has taken meaningful school reform to scale. The district has made this remarkable transition under the leadership of Jerry Weast, a creative superintendent with a gift for deep thinking and plain talk. From the outside, it is easy to misinterpret the MCPS story as one of a heroic leader driving a top-down change effort. It is true that Weast is a highly effective executive, but *Leading for Equity* tells a more complex story of the sometimes contentious journey the entire Montgomery County community has been on since 1999.

ORGANIZATION OF *LEADING FOR EQUITY*

Before writing *Leading for Equity*, each of us studied a number of school districts over the years and wrote case studies and articles about what we learned from them. We all have a connection to MCPS—two of us have followed its progress since 2003 through our work as faculty with the Public Education Leadership Project at Harvard University, and the third has observed its efforts as an education author and citizen of Montgomery County. As we considered how best to communicate its journey, we had many discussions about whether to tell its story chronologically or thematically. In the end, we decided to organize the chapters according to themes, which means that each chapter has its own timeline, and the reader will go back and forth in time throughout the book. This approach helped us to not simply tell the story, but to make sense of it.

Chapters 1 through 4 lay the foundation of the district's work by telling the story of its strategy, stakeholder relationships, and human capital investments; and chapters 5 and 6 build on that foundation and tie the story together. Chapter 7 offers six lessons from its journey, and chapter 8 provides a framework that other districts can use to apply the lessons.

Chapter 1 describes the context of MCPS in 1999 when Jerry Weast arrived, along with his efforts to engage the community in a problem analysis and strategy development process. The district's performance data told the story of a widening achievement gap between rich and poor, immigrant and nonimmigrant, native English speaker and nonnative English speaker, and between whites and Asians on the one hand and Hispanics and African Americans on the other. The county's residential patterns led to identifiable areas where achievement was predictably lower based on the demographics of its neighborhoods. Weast worked with his team, the board, and stakeholders from around the district and the community to raise standards for all students by setting an overarching goal—a "North Star"—of readiness for college and high-wage work. Their plan was to eventually close the achievement gap among subgroups of students by raising the bar for every child, including those already at the top of the performance curve, even as they accelerated performance for students who were academically behind. In a dramatic departure from business as usual at MCPS, the team proposed to allocate more resources to schools with student populations that were academically underperforming, the premise being that if students who were behind were going to be expected to meet a rigorous standard, they would need more time and more support in order to catch up. Chapter 1 tells the story of the MCPS team's efforts to challenge the status quo in order to "raise the bar and close the gap."

Chapter 2 explains the rationale behind the MCPS strategy and its early implementation. The strategy was based on the idea of "differentiation" of resources and instructional approaches based on needs, coupled with common, rigorous standards across the entire district. When Weast arrived in 1999, the Montgomery County neighborhoods with high-minority and low-income populations had the lowest-performing schools, while the predominantly white and higher-income region of Montgomery County had some of nation's best schools. Weast did not back away from pointing out the contrast, but rather highlighted it by dividing MCPS into two zones, red and green. Weast made the argument that distributing resources equitably meant differentiated allocation, not equal distribution to all schools. In the new strategy, Red Zone schools would receive more support and resources than Green Zone schools because their students needed more time and support to catch up. The plan was controversial and met resistance from the community at first, but Weast and his team stood firm and eventually won sufficient support for the Red Zone/Green Zone approach.

At the same time, MCPS introduced a strategy to improve student achievement across all grades by connecting content standards from kindergarten through twelfth grade and aligning them with the knowledge and skills students need for success in advanced courses in high school. The end result was a "Pathway to Success" that students could follow throughout their schooling on the way to excellent college and career outcomes. Chapter 2 details the efforts to backward map the content standards from high school to kindergarten and align the curriculum in all grades to these standards, as well an initial focus on two areas—early-grade reading and high school advanced courses—in order to bookend the reform efforts while encouraging teachers to differentiate their delivery of the common curriculum to help all students meet the rigorous standards.

Chapter 3 sheds light on Weast's efforts to blur the lines between governance and management by creating deep relationships with the school board, the employee unions, and other key stakeholders, which ultimately increased the district's capacity to improve and created a shared accountability for results. He insisted that the presidents of the three unions be full participants in the development and implementation of the improvement strategy. Eventually, the union leaders joined the executive leadership team. Even though they continued to disagree on important issues, Weast and the union leadership were able to create a respectful and collaborative relationship that led to innovative teacher work agreements.

At the same time, Weast and his leadership team worked closely with the school board and county council on the development and funding of the improvement strategy and then followed up with results so strong that the two publicly elected bodies supported the team consistently for nearly a decade. Parents and the business community were engaged as well, and chapter 3 illustrates how capacity and accountability increased through these stakeholder relationships.

MCPS had a core belief that behind every successful student was a stream of exceptional teachers, support staff, and outstanding principals. As chapter 4 shows, MCPS invested in its employees at all levels, from senior executives to teachers and principals to bus drivers, in ways that were consistent with its improvement strategy. These investments came in the form of professional development focused on building the skills and knowledge people needed to be successful in implementing the strategy. Unable to do everything at once, the district first made significant investments in building the instructional capacity of teachers in the lowest-performing Red Zone schools, rolling it out to the remaining Red Zone schools and all Green Zone schools later.

The unions and the district worked together to create a professional growth system for all employees, beginning with teachers. The system included compensation schedules, performance-based career paths, and a mechanism for removing low performers from the system. The district and unions also worked together to create a year-long learning institute for school-based teams that would study case studies of MCPS schools that had achieved success with the differentiation strategy and apply the case lessons to their own work by creating and implementing action plans for their own schools with the support of institute staff. The district's many strategic investments in the knowledge and skill of its people have paid off dramatically through results for students.

Once the strategy was under way and investments in stakeholder relationships and staff capacity were in progress, the leadership team began to think about how to knit the entire district together in a way that would help the various initiatives work in concert with the improvement strategy. They created a new set of systems and structures that reinforced the new behaviors that were necessary to improve the performance of students and accelerate those who were farthest behind. Chapter 5 describes these efforts, including a rearrangement of the top leadership structure in MCPS that created community superintendents who oversaw clusters of schools and reported to the chief performance officer. Weast relied on the new configuration to drive the implementation of other strategic initiatives. These included the full deployment of a strategic planning process based on the well-respected Baldrige quality system, and an accountability and organizational learning system modeled on the New York City Police Department's CompStat model. They also invested heavily in technology, including classroom tools that helped teachers more effectively diagnose and respond to student learning needs in real time.

Weast and his team also began to dismantle systems that "sorted" students away from rigorous content beginning very early in their academic careers. In their place they created new systems, such as a Mathematics Pathway, which opened up access to higher-level math content to all students by committing to creating the capacity for 80 percent of all students to complete algebra by the end of eighth grade, a key gateway to advanced math in high school. Chapter 5 describes how these efforts helped accelerate the effectiveness of MCPS's differentiation strategy.

In the first few years of Weast's superintendency, the efforts of the MCPS team resulted in gains in student achievement. But the story from the first five chapters—crafting a sound academic strategy, building stakeholder relationships, investing in people, and aligning systems and structures—has its limitations. Chapter 6 describes how Weast and his team recognized that they had to do even more to improve the performance of minority and low-income students if they were to have the same access to college and career success as students from the more affluent areas of the county. Though some Red Zone schools, such as Broad Acres, Viers Mill, and Piney Branch, had proved that their students could perform as well as any others in MCPS, the progress was not widely distributed enough. Weast and his team began to realize that the beliefs that many staff members held about the ability of students from various backgrounds to perform at high levels was the next frontier of change. The team decided to explicitly address how beliefs about race and achievement influence the behavior of teachers and students. In a leadership meeting with hundreds of principals and central office staff after Hurricane Katrina struck New Orleans in August 2005, Weast was transparent about the new focus, saying, "I am going to get right down into the race issue, and I am going to talk about *Hispanic* and *African American*. And if it hurts, I'm sorry. I apologize respectfully, but I am going to talk about it. You need to talk about it. You need to have that [conversation] because we are going to [work] together to destroy institutional barriers that have sorted kids for way too long."[2]

Chapter 6 chronicles the leadership team's work following the Katrina speech to help schools focus more directly on the difficult issues of race and achievement. These efforts included sharpening the focus of accountability and learning systems, creating tools for principals and community superintendents to more accurately identify minority students for high-level courses, and providing professional development experiences that blended conversations about beliefs and behaviors with skill-building work on instructional practices. The chapter ends with a look at MCPS's current work in this area as it continues to try to accelerate the performance of all students in the system.

The overarching evidence from MCPS is that all children can achieve academic success. And as a rising tide lifts all boats, MCPS provides evidence that school improvement—in both policy and practice—works to the advantage of the community as a whole. The MCPS story will resonate in any school district that is interested in high achievement for all students. Chapter 7 explains six central lessons that emerge from the story for parents, politicians, teachers, and administrators and policy makers:

1. Implementing a strategy of common, rigorous standards with differentiated resources and instruction can create excellence and equity for all students.

2. Adopting a "value chain" approach to the K–12 continuum increases quality and provides a logical frame for strategic choices.

3. Blurring the lines between governance, management, staff, and community increases capacity and accountability.

4. Creating systems and structures that change behaviors is a way to shift beliefs if they lead to student learning gains.

5. Breaking the link between race, ethnicity, and student outcomes is difficult without confronting the effect that beliefs about race and ethnicity have on student learning.

6. Leading for equity matters.

With the lessons explained, chapter 8 provides a concrete framework for leaders who are interested in using MCPS's approach to strategy development and implementation. The problem-solving approach to strategy was developed as a tool for district leadership teams and stakeholders to use in diagnosing and responding to performance and organizational problems. Developed out of the Public Education Leadership Project at Harvard University, the framework is already used by a number of district- and school-level leadership teams. Grounded in the continuous improvement literature, the tool has seven steps:

1. Identify and analyze the problem.

2. Develop a theory of action.

3. Design a strategy.

4. Plan for implementation.

5. Implement.

6. Assess progress.

7. Adapt and modify for continuous improvement.

This final chapter includes definitions for each of the steps, guiding questions that teams can use to put the tool into practice, and examples from MCPS that help illuminate each step.

A COMPELLING MODEL

Because public education has had little success in realizing high levels of academic achievement at scale, the story this book tells is all the more important. Pockets of excellence exist, but as noted earlier, access to rigorous and demanding coursework is largely predictable by race, ethnicity, and family income. *Leading for Equity* reveals a clear path to improving schools and making access to college or satisfying work a reality for all. In the process of working to close achievement and opportunity gaps, education leaders struggle with key questions:

- Where should we start?

- What are the economic and political dynamics that we must account for in our strategy, and what impact might they have on our ability to implement?

- How should we organize curriculum and instruction to achieve results from kindergarten through twelfth grade?

- How can we differentiate our strategy in order to bring reform to scale?

- What investments should we make in our people, and what systems and tools do they need to be successful?

- How should progress be measured and communicated?

- How can early improvements be accelerated and sustained?

This short book provides a frame for these questions by highlighting key action areas in the MCPS improvement process. Each is illuminated with stories that illustrate the hard work of reform in a meaningful way.

Leading for Equity is not a lament but a celebration. It does more than describe the achievement gap; it offers vivid examples of organizational change that works, as well as bumps in the road and how they were overcome. While the changes that unfold in this narrative are undergirded by theory, this book is above all practical. It tells the story of concrete changes that worked in a real school district with real people. Not a conventional how-to book, it nonetheless lays out the architecture of lasting change. And while the activities and changes described here should not be slavishly copied, the lessons are universal.

Demographers predict that by 2050 the U.S. population will be over 50 percent Hispanic and African American, the very students who are currently systematically underserved. It is in no one's interest to leave these children behind. Our future as a nation depends on their success; we are all in it together. Achievement and opportunity gaps are deeply rooted in our antiquated system of public education that was designed to educate only certain segments of the population. As society works to build equity and opportunity for all children, we must directly address and radically change institutionalized practices that perpetuate inequity. *Leading for Equity* shows how committed educators and a mobilized community can create policies and practices that do just that.

CHAPTER ONE

Challenging the Status Quo

[Weast's] focus on the moral imperative—that one group of children should not be consigned to schools that were substandard while a relative handful of children in excellent schools were flourishing— was the basis for a strategy that would blend *equity* and *rigor* in equal measure.

Great opportunities often come disguised as insoluble problems. When Jerry Weast arrived in Montgomery County in 1999, the school board gave him a mandate to dramatically improve performance, especially for students who had historically not been served well by the district. The gaps between students of different races, ethnicities, and family incomes were wide and entrenched, and many talented, committed educators had worked on closing them for years. But neither the board nor the community had a full picture of the dramatic shifts in assumptions, strategy, and education practices it would take to create the necessary change.

Weast's first challenge was to identify existing barriers to high performance for all students and develop some working hypotheses about their causes, and then propose an approach for tackling the barriers that the entire community could embrace. This required building shared understanding of the purposes for which children would be educated, the standards necessary for ensuring that all students could attain those purposes, and a blueprint for action to move from the current condition toward a new shared vision of success for every child. It also required a blunt and clear-eyed assessment of why performance disparities existed in the first place.

A LONG, COMPLICATED HISTORY

The achievement gaps in Montgomery County in 1999 were not a new phenomenon. For more than four decades, MCPS had wrestled with the issues of race and the low performance of specific student groups, recent immigrants, racial minorities, and the poor in particular. The difference was that minority populations in the district had been small enough that they had a minimal impact on overall perceptions of performance in the district. Because of demographic changes in the 1980s and '90s, the disparities became more apparent.

Before *Brown v. Board of Education* was handed down in 1954, Montgomery County had two separate school systems, one for African American students and one for white students. Separate and unequal, the schools with African American students received fewer resources than the white schools. One month after the landmark *Brown* decision, the Montgomery County Board of Education appointed a committee of administrators to develop an integration implementation plan, but the district was slow to desegregate, leading the NAACP to repeatedly criticize the board for perpetuating inequities between the races.

By 1980, demographics had changed. Newer immigrant populations made up primarily of Asians, Africans, and Hispanics had moved into the county, and the total minority population had doubled. In a new political climate, board members who had opposed "social engineering" removed some busing plans and disbanded the board's minority relations committee.

The board also attempted to shut down several integrated schools, but community members challenged the plan, and the Maryland State Board of Education stepped in to halt the closures. In response, MCPS created magnet programs in schools with large numbers of minorities to attract white students and also used race-based admissions as a way to integrate other schools. The number of minority students continued to grow, and even though many attended schools with magnet programs, most did not participate in the advanced academic programs offered there. Minority leaders in the community became vocal opponents of the magnet schools, saying they served only white students, further contributing to the achievement gap.

In spite of the changing demographics and the struggle with race relations in the district, MCPS was still considered to be one of the best school districts in the nation. Students in affluent areas of the county received a high-quality education and consistently scored well on standardized tests. But in 1990, the school board commissioned Yale University professor Edmund Gordon to study minority student achievement. The study, known as *The Gordon Report*, confirmed that the district "need[ed] several more elements for the improvement of minority students . . . it was widely perceived that teachers and other school staff members tended to have low expectations of minority students and tended to invest less effort in the academic support and challenge of minority students."[1]

In response, African American superintendent Paul Vance implemented a program of action—Success for Every Student (SES)—to address the issues, when he assumed the superintendency in 1991. Vance had worked on integration and achievement gap issues for many years as a deputy superintendent in MCPS and Baltimore. His team had included specific language about addressing the needs of minority students in their original SES plan, but the board had refused to approve it until the rhetoric was changed to focus on "all students." Staff members at the time were disappointed with this refusal to publicly acknowledge that race was a significant issue in the schools. From the spring of 1992 to the end of 1999, the district implemented the approved initiatives. However, despite well-intentioned efforts on the part of administration and staff, the achievement gap persisted; there was very little improvement in minority student test scores. Most of the activities were programs aimed at particular student groups, without an overarching strategy for improving teaching and learning across the district. Although white and Asian students, on average, maintained some of the highest performance levels in the state, the data showed lack of academic progress for African American and Hispanic children.

In 1997, a committee was commissioned to study progress under Success for Every Student. *The Larson Report*, as it is known, highlighted gaps in achievement. The authors found that race and class could largely predict academic success. Most significantly, researchers found that by third grade, educators could determine which students would go on to participate in honors and advanced placement (AP) courses.

In 1999, a *Washington Post* article uncovered a vast grading disparity across the district. Schools with high African American and Hispanic populations were giving children passing grades, when similar scores across town would have earned a D. The lack of standardization in grading and curriculum—which was made public in the article—highlighted the critical need to find a workable solution to the growing problems within the district.

Almost exactly ten years after the release of *The Gordon Report*, Vance elected to retire at the end of his second contract. The Montgomery County Board of Education conducted an extensive search for a superintendent and in 1999 unanimously selected Jerry Weast, the superintendent of Guilford County (Greensboro), North Carolina. Weast was raised on a farm in Moran, Kansas. His father farmed all his life, and his mother taught in a one-room schoolhouse before Weast and his three siblings were born. Throughout his career, Weast's rural upbringing influenced his communication style. Those who worked with him marveled at his seemingly limitless supply of analogies based on farm life, such as comparing incremental change to putting a new coat of paint on a rickety barn instead of tearing it down and building a new one.

Weast got his first job at age fourteen and worked his way through Allen County Community College in Iola, Kansas, earning an associate's degree in business and then a bachelor's in business education with a concentration in accounting from Pittsburg State University in Pittsburg, Kansas. Rather than entering the corporate world like most of his classmates, Weast took a job teaching accounting and psychology and coaching football at a local high school. The rest, as they say, is history. After three years, he worked his way up to principal of the school, and a few years later took his first superintendency. He ran a number of districts in Kansas before earning his doctoral degree in education from Oklahoma State University. He subsequently served as superintendent in Great Falls, Montana; Durham County, North Carolina; and Sioux Falls, South Dakota, before taking the Guilford County job in Greensboro, North Carolina. Throughout his career, he was known for having a deep understanding of teaching and learning as well as organizational management, and for having an innovative approach to using technology to improve the efficiency and effectiveness of his districts. In Guilford County, he engaged in a number of efforts to open up opportunities for minority students, and was known in particular for expanding the number of students enrolled in advanced placement courses. With his track record of addressing equity issues, the MCPS board gave him a mandate to raise student achievement across the board, regardless of race, ethnicity, and socioeconomic factors.

GETTING STARTED: ASSESSING THE PROBLEM

Montgomery County is located on the western border of the nation's capital. It is not only the state's most populous county; it is the state's most affluent. But in addition to the older, established neighborhoods and the new subdivisions, in 1999 there were deep pockets of poverty—a situation that is even truer today. Over the previous decade, the makeup of the student population had changed dramatically. In 1990, 52 percent of MPCS students were white; by 1999, the white student population had shrunk by 10 percent, while the overall student population had increased by 21 percent.

In order to get to know the district after he was hired, Weast literally "rode the bus," hitchhiking with the early-morning mail run as it left headquarters for the district's two hundred–plus mail stops. Up close and personal, in late summer 1999, Weast "discovered" a district within a district. Once upon a time, Montgomery County had been a racially homogeneous affluent area. Indeed, that had been its brand. No longer.

Today Montgomery County is heterogeneous—racially, socially, and economically. In the mid-1980s, the district was predominantly white. In 2008, the district had about one hundred and forty thousand students, more than 60 percent of whom were racial or ethnic minorities, with burgeoning numbers of poor and nonnative English-speaking students. Students came from more than 163 countries and spoke 134 different languages. And the bitter truth is that, across the nation, these characteristics have strong predictive power. Typically, they are harbingers of low expectations and poor academic performance.

Weast's reading of the data, combined with his school-visiting blitz, convinced him that there were two Montgomery Counties, one nested within the other. One area was largely urban, surrounding municipal centers and major transportation arteries, stretching from one end of the county to nearly the other, beginning at the border with Washington, D.C. Weast called it the Red Zone. Everything outside of it he called the Green Zone (see figure 1.1). The Red Zone was made up primarily of immigrant families, Hispanics and African Americans, many of whom were living in poverty. The performance of students in this area was far below the academic performance of the students in the Green Zone. It was only a matter of time before the weight of the Red Zone's inequalities engulfed the Green Zone, which would have a profound effect on the county's traditionally high average test scores.

To Weast, the realization that the county was failing to educate large number of students, and consequently families as a whole, was surprising and simply unacceptable. He used this information to reach out to stakeholders in the community—stressing the sense of urgency he felt about the need to solve the issue of the achievement gap. Describing the situation, Weast said, "The only thing we could predict was failure, with a great deal of consistency. We could also predict who would fail, because the evidence didn't show any substantive type of *systemic* approach to raising the level of education in our high-poverty schools."[2]

FIGURE 1.1   *Red and Green schools*

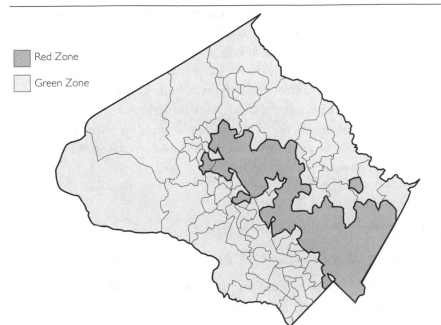

Red Zone

Green Zone

ESTABLISHING A VISION AND SETTING GOALS

Weast and his executive team knew that to bring about full-scale, wide-ranging reform, they had to take an honest look at the causes of academic disparities in Montgomery County. Not only did they have to define the problems and present them to the community; they had to collectively assume responsibility for the system's failures and set new goals. A piecemeal approach to problem solving might help some students, but it would do nothing to address the equity issues that affected the system as a whole. MCPS needed a goal that everyone could rally around and that could anchor a systemic and coherent reform strategy.

Weast and his team believed that the twenty-first century's economic realities had already established the school district's goal, its North Star. Readiness for college and high-wage work was the standard to which all graduates would be held. Historically, public schools acted on the premise that there were two, even three sets of graduation standards: one set for the college-bound, one for the vocationally inclined, and a third never-never land diploma called general education. But the MCPS team was convinced that these distinctions no longer made sense, if indeed they ever had; in today's world, work readiness and college standards are one and the same. This assumption dictated one set of rigorous academic standards for all students and specific benchmarks to measure minimum readiness for college and high-wage work:

- A score of 1650-plus on the SAT or

- A score of 24-plus on the ACT test

- Demonstrated success in AP courses and exams or

- Successful completion of an International Baccalaureate (IB) program

If they were to adopt this standard as their North Star, Weast and his team needed to ask a number of important questions:

- How can we create world-class schools that give all students access to a rigorous education that will make them college and work ready by the time they graduate?

- How should we best tackle the issue of racial disparity in academic achievement?

- Under what conditions can we change long-established trends in outcomes?

- What is our strategy for creating those conditions?

- How will we measure achievement and mastery?

Weast and his team did not have all the answers, but these questions guided their engagement with the community and their early work to create a strategy to challenge the status quo. They did not spend significant time planning to change things that were outside their sphere of influence. For instance, they acknowledged that they could not change their students' socioeconomic status but committed to changing school and district factors that were in their control in order to bring the quality of education in the Red Zone up to that in the Green Zone.

A CALL TO ACTION

Over a period of three months in the fall of 1999, district and school staff, consultants, board members, and citizens (a group that numbered in the hundreds) worked together to analyze the critical issues facing the school system. They organized into various committees and convened meetings and conferences on a range of relevant topics that brought the community together. They assembled research and examples of best practices, and committees used these findings to recommend a strategy to raise student performance and close the achievement gap.

At the conclusion of the period of data mining in the fall of 1999, Weast and his team gathered to write a blueprint for change. They wanted to communicate to the people of Montgomery County the sense of urgency they felt about the state of education in the district and the desperate need for reform.

Entitled *Our Call to Action: Raising the Bar and Closing the Gap*, the report was the hallmark of Weast's first few months in office. Staff characterized the report as a "plan to plan" rather than a fully developed recipe for success. While no one would have predicted it at the time, the report would serve as a foundation for the MCPS strategy over the next decade.

Building on earlier work in the district and Vance's Success for Every Student program, the report contained specific academic milestones for the district, including some related to racial disparities, such as encouraging larger numbers of students from each racial and ethnic group to participate in the SAT; reducing the suspension rates of African American and Hispanic students; and eliminating the disproportionate number of African American students in special education programs.

It identified six "trend benders," or concrete steps MCPS could take to change conditions in schools so that downward performance trends would begin to bend upward:

1. Developing a system of shared accountability

2. Workforce excellence through targeted training and action research

3. Broadening the concept of literacy

4. Family and community partnerships

5. Organizational excellence—reorganizing assets for school success

6. Integrated quality management and data-driven decision making

The report reflected the best thinking of the community that had emerged during the data mining work and included supportive quotes from a wide range of stakeholders. Henry Quintero, director of the Latino Civil Rights Task Force of Maryland, offered, "We support the Call to Action to raise the achievement of students and close the gap of Hispanic and African American students. We're behind the superintendent and board of education 100 percent."[3] Linna Barnes, president of the Montgomery County PTA, added, "All children achieve more when families become involved in their children's education. The efforts to increase parent and family involvement will go a long way toward closing the achievement gap and improving the education of all students."[4]

The plan proposed developing a new curriculum and systematically linking quality standards for teaching, learning, support, and progress monitoring—of teachers, students, and administrators. Building on some of the teachers union ongoing work, specific components of the plan outlined ways to think about and change teaching by creating a culture where teachers critiqued each other's work and investigated best practices together. The report also touched on the impact of adult expectations on student performance and pushed for the development of a fact-based accountability system that focused on student learning. It proposed that academic milestones and student performance measures should be linked to a staff evaluation. The report also envisioned accountability as part of the daily work of students. Students and families would use self-assessments to chart their progress in achieving goals and to identify areas that needed improvement.

Embedded in *Our Call to Action* was a new vision of shared accountability and a shared governance structure. It called for the collaboration of parents, the general public, county and state government, colleges and universities, advocacy groups and civic organizations, and the business community in order to be successful. It attempted to make reform a priority for the whole community and was designed to present the early reform ideas in a way that gave all of the stakeholders a sense of ownership of the change process. The report put forth the innovative idea that everyone involved in public education should play a part in leadership and in problem resolution. Joint ownership of the system by the board, unions, staff, and community groups meant shared responsibility for decision making as well as joint ownership of outcomes and results. Weast believed that blurring the lines between leadership and governance would diffuse former antagonisms and encourage everyone to work together in a collaborative process. In fact, *Our Call to Action* made the point that the process of employee contract negotiations, the capital budget, the capital improvement plan, and the operating budget would all interact and be critical in identifying and accessing the resources needed for the ideas contained in the document.

As Isiah Leggett, then president of the Montgomery County Council (the body that funds MCPS), remarked at the time, "The single most important issue that we must resolve is raising the level of achievement for all students. We have a diverse population, but we don't want diverse levels of expectation or education. Every student deserves the same opportunity for high standards of teaching, available resources, and equal expectations of academic results."[5]

CLARIFYING ASSUMPTIONS

Our Call to Action proposed a goal for the district that could be paraphrased as "Greening the Red Zone." In order to reach the goal, the team felt it was necessary to put forward six key assumptions, each of which challenged the status quo. The overarching message was that business as usual was no longer acceptable.

- First, policy makers could not mandate change. Change would only come about through local capacity and local will. To that end, resources had to be reorganized to help instructional staff—teachers, support staff, and administrators—to act in new ways.

- Second, there must be an end to the culture of blame. A new environment had to be created, one that valued risk taking, recognition, and shared accountability.

- Third, because quality of teaching makes *all* the difference in the children's experience, resources should support teaching and learning. Further, the workforce should strengthen itself and integrate research and practice into its activities.

- Fourth, antiquated structures and institutional systems were in large part responsible for current failures. As a result, school quality discussions should focus on new factors: class size, student groupings, attitudes and expectations, dispute resolution, and family involvement.

- Fifth, it was up to the whole community to participate in the *Call to Action*. The authors acknowledged that there was not a consensus on the ideas for reform, and it was up to the people of Montgomery County to flesh out ideas, identify key problems, quantify them with data, and examine possible strategies.

- And finally, MCPS should be guided in its reform choices by findings from research and by decisions and suggestions made by those closest to the problem—in other words, principals and teachers. It was important to be able to evaluate ideas to determine whether or not they were successful. The success or failure of a reform strategy ultimately depends on what happens in thousands of individual classrooms. Without the buy-in and support of an entire organization and the people it serves (parents and children), change will not take place. If teachers feel genuine involvement with their task and feel a sense of ownership and accountability, change will occur.

Our Call to Action wisely concluded, "We do not have all the answers. But like many of the most vexing problems we have faced in Montgomery County, the answers are likely to be among us."[6] It was released with the expectation that annual reports to stakeholders would detail progress and adjustments to the plan.

MOBILIZING COMMUNITY SUPPORT

Bringing the community on board with this vision involved a massive public relations effort. Weast and his team worked to craft his messages and to develop video and slide presentations. By speaking with small groups of people across the community, chatting informally with families, and going through data in a simple but compelling way, the executive leadership team made the case for reform.

One of the most politically sensitive issues in *Our Call to Action* was the idea of using resources equitably rather than equally. The problem analysis indicated that the district was poorly designed to ensure a high-quality education experience in every neighborhood, because of significant problems in the allocation of financial and human resources. MCPS had been distributing resources nearly equally across all schools, regardless of performance. To address the problems in the Red Zone schools, the team proposed that more resources be allocated to them so that the quality of education would increase to the same level as that in the Green Zone schools. This concept was met in some quarters with suspicion and mistrust, and generated resistance and pushback from parts of the community. Some parents in wealthier parts of the county did not like the idea of forgoing resources in their area so that additional funds could be invested in lower-performing schools. They were concerned that their children would be shortchanged in the process and that overall performance across the district would go down. Red Zone parents had their concerns as well. Then–board member Sharon Cox, a Green Zone resident who had previously been president of the Montgomery County Council of PTAs, recalled the tensions: "The concern in the community was (about) how can you both raise the bar and close the gap. People in the wealthier sections of Montgomery County, identified as 'green' were afraid that all resources would to the needier or 'red' area. People in the red area were afraid they wouldn't get the attention they needed because of the raising the bar issues in the green area. And I remember . . . saying that the expectation is that while we're increasing achievement levels and working to fulfill every child's potential, children with more dramatic barriers would improve at a faster rate than the other students who were already up there."[7]

In the face of skepticism, the team pressed ahead with the message. At the time, a union official who asked to remain anonymous said in a *Washington Post* article, "There was a great deal of denial before Weast . . . Some of it was believing your own propaganda. We always had a group of kids you could hang the world-class system on. And you could kind of close your eyes and not see the other school system. Dr. Weast came and said we can't just not see it anymore."[8]

Through endless outreach visits, town meetings, and presentations, Weast and his team were able to communicate a moral imperative that the community eventually recognized. In a feat that has been profoundly difficult in public education, Weast was able to convince enough people that resources should be distributed for equity because *it was the right thing to do.*

He also convinced people that *it was the smart thing to do* economically. As academic achievement rose in all parts of the county, home values would rise, employers would increasingly see the area as a good place to create jobs, and the overall health of the community would improve. Together, these twin imperatives—the right thing and the smart thing—would guide the work of district staff, the board, and the community.

Weast's communication style—unassuming and colloquial—was a sharp contrast to the controversial ideas he was proposing. He was not afraid to talk explicitly about race and ethnicity. Some members of his leadership team recalled that, at first, his forthright discussions of the district's African American and Hispanic students being short-changed by the system were often met with stunned silence by white business leaders and county power brokers unaccustomed to hearing another white man talk in those terms. Deputy superintendent Frieda Lacey had worked in the district since 1971 in a variety of roles, including teacher, principal, and multiple central office roles. In that time, she had seen many efforts to address the achievement gap. As an African American educator, she had observed a range of responses from the community over the years to efforts to address the achievement gap. She drew a contrast between Weast and former superintendents, saying, "What made it different for Dr. Weast was that he was 'one of them.' It is like a family member saying we have a problem within our family."[9]

Armed with the powerful visual aid of the Red and Green Zones, Weast was able to very publicly demonstrate how MCPS was not meeting the needs of all students. The map clearly showed the pattern linking poor achievement to highly impacted schools. It was a dramatic tool that caught the attention of everyone in the community. To garner support for his idea, Weast met with a variety of stakeholders, including union leaders, members of the business community, teachers, parents, and administrators, asking for their input, counsel, and recommendations.

Our Call to Action was presented in a series of back-to-back regional meetings with principals and their staffs at the end of the school day and at community meetings in the evenings. After community presentations, Weast and his team of facilitators would break into small groups with the audience to discuss questions and continue the dialogue. In addition, Weast gave presentations for different segments of community, presentations translated into multiple Asian languages and Spanish, for example. And Weast was fair game for questions and comments: not everyone was enthusiastic, but he stood his ground. Through countless presentations and discussions, the message that people needed to work collaboratively to improve the schools began to work its way into the community's collective conscience. Although not everyone agreed with the specifics or with the pace of change, it was a first step to creating unity of purpose.

DEFENDING RIGOROUS STANDARDS

With a new North Star—college and work readiness as measured on a number of dimensions, including achievement on standardized tests—Weast and his team would eventually create standards in several content areas from kindergarten through high school that would ensure that students were well prepared.

These standards were dramatically more aggressive than the definition of *proficient* that the state of Maryland adopted in the wake of the No Child Left Behind (NCLB) Act. As Weast describes it, the state standards are a minimum level of acceptability, not a goal to aspire to. Describing the state standards as baseball sized, Weast declared that the new MCPS standards needed to be basketball sized to ensure that students had more than basic skills, but were instead prepared for college and high-wage work. With the above definition of *college and work ready*, the MCPS executive team set a goal: 80 percent of graduates would meet the internal standard by 2014. If the district aimed for these goals, state test scores would take care of themselves without an explicit focus on preparing students for the exams. In the beginning, though, Weast and his team had to build momentum for the changes that would be necessary for successful implementation.

Resistance emerged from teachers and parents alike. Many felt that the new standards were too hard for students to reach and too hard for teachers to teach. But the board and the leadership team held fast and continued to present their vision for a school of the future, where all children succeed and teachers rise to the challenge by providing their students with the education they need to reach their goals.

One frequent argument was that not all children would attend college, so the focus on rigorous standards was unnecessary for them. Of course this was true, but for too long in MCPS college going was highly predictable by race and income. High standards would open up the gateway to college for every student. But even if students chose different paths, Weast often told stories of a world of work so dramatically changed, it is almost unrecognizable to our grandparents. Look at the place where your car is serviced, he would say. Mechanics use computers to assess problems. They need to be independent thinkers. They must also be technologically sophisticated enough to understand and diagnose discrete problems. Mechanics need communication skills to order parts and to talk with customers. What is true for mechanics, plumbers, and carpenters is true throughout the traditional blue-collar world. Consider nursing and the sheer volume of technology-based equipment that nurses use on a daily basis. Patient records are on computers, monitoring systems are computerized, and nurses must be able to read, understand, and respond to complicated data. Because of this, Weast argued, our children must be able to finish high school ready to move into this increasingly complex world. Over time, teachers and parents became more invested in the North Star and the blueprint for reaching it, but the journey was bumpy at times. In subsequent chapters, we will explore the twists and turns along the way.

CONCLUSION

America can meet the competitive challenge it faces if its citizens can agree on a national approach similar to the one the MCPS community has adopted: reduce variability while improving overall quality by agreeing to a set of common, high standards in a few important areas, creating a system in which teachers and students have the support they need to reach those standards and be successful. The majority of staff and stakeholders in Montgomery County have come to believe that all students are *entitled* to the same rigorous academic education. Weast strongly believes that children should not be sorted into vocational or general tracks, but rather they should all be given the foundations for academic mastery. This belief has permeated the district. His focus on the moral imperative—that one group of children should not be consigned to schools that were substandard while a relative handful of children in excellent schools were flourishing—was the basis for a strategy that would blend *equity* and *rigor* in equal measure. This vision has enabled MCPS to make significant progress in closing the achievement gap in less than a decade.

Many districts have a document such as *Our Call to Action*, and superintendents often use community meetings and stakeholder task forces to build momentum in the early days of their leadership. One difference in Montgomery County is that leaders at all levels—board members, community organizations, teachers, principals, parents—committed to the "plan to plan" over the long term rather than moving from one issue to another without regard to the work done in the original plan. Another difference is that MCPS *actually implemented* the ideas in *Our Call to Action* and allowed the elements of the plan to evolve over time as it learned more about what worked and what did not, rather than throwing out the plan every couple of years and starting over.

But the task is ongoing. As late as 2005, five years into the implementation of the Red Zone strategy, a board member reported a comment by Green Zone parent: "Those children don't need an all-day kindergarten, they've got Head Start." The board member's reply? "It's not about equity of resources; it's about equity of opportunities. If you believe your children are challenged to their fullest potential, then the resources we are putting into these other areas aren't taking away from your children."[10]

The catalyst for change described in this chapter began the MCPS journey that continues today. Having outlined the North Star and some guiding principles, how did MCPS push the agenda forward? How did Weast and the team develop an academic strategy that would allow them to begin making progress without trying to do everything at once? The next chapter describes the differentiation strategy and the first phase of its implementation.

CHAPTER TWO

Implementing a Differentiation Strategy

[In reality,] unequal treatment is sometimes required to provide equal opportunity. In plain English, more money, more talent, and more time were essential if the Red Zone students could be expected to rapidly meet the same standards as Green Zone students.

Our Call to Action expressed a new vision and the broad outlines of a strategy to improve overall student performance and to close the achievement gap. The report was widely supported by various community stakeholders, union leaders, board members, parents, and teachers. Once the idea had taken hold that differentiated resources and instructional approaches across schools should be need based, the team was able to turn its attention to an important question. Since the goal was established—college and work readiness—where should reform begin?

The catalysts for this decision were two important facts Weast and his team recognized about student achievement in MCPS. One was the differences in performance between students in Red Zone and Green Zone schools. The other came as a result of an internal research report that found a high correlation between grade 3 literacy and high school honors course enrollment. Most importantly, the correlation was equally strong across all four major racial and ethnic groups in MCPS.

After reviewing this report, Weast decided that the only way to change achievement patterns predicted by race and income was to implement reform at both ends of the K–12 continuum, with emphasis on the neediest schools. And by starting at each end, Weast and his team could force the middle to change as well. Mapping backward from high school, the district set benchmarks for achievement starting in kindergarten that would prepare children for higher-level coursework through the next twelve grades.

Interventions that included raising standards, introducing a common curriculum, and providing smaller class sizes in K–2 and a full-day kindergarten would maximize the number of students who graduated ready to compete in college without remediation. Focusing high school student outcomes on selected targets would increase the participation of minority students in the SAT and advanced placement (AP) exams. Beginning with a curriculum overhaul and moving on to putting in place new supports in selected high-poverty elementary schools, Weast and his staff began a journey to raise student achievement across the district.

RED ZONE/GREEN ZONE

Dividing MCPS into distinct zones did more than highlight the correlation between low-performing schools and high-minority populations; it formed the foundation of MCPS's strategy. The zones allowed MCPS to target resources where they were most needed and do it in a way that respected the uniqueness of each school. As Weast said:

> My first approach was to define the problem and try to understand the issues we were working on before looking for solutions. Then the question became, what do you do if 75–80% of all minority students live in a well-defined geographical area, 75–80% of all poverty is in that same area, 75–80% of all students learning English are in that same area, and disproportionately lower student performance occurs across that same geographical area? What do you do when that same geographical area includes more than 67,000 students, the equivalent of the 53rd largest school district in the nation, and the poverty rate in Kindergarten is 50% and growing?[1]

Each zone accounted for roughly the same number of students, around seventy thousand, but had drastically different demographics. As we described in chapter 1, students in the Green Zone were predominantly white and came from middle- to high-income families; those in the Red Zone were mostly African American and Hispanic, low income, and English language learners. Furthermore, Green Zone schools consistently scored 20 points higher on standardized assessments, enrolled more students in honors and AP courses, and had higher college attainment than Red Zone schools. In reality, MCPS was two school districts within one.

As Weast and his team saw it, if predictable variability among schools was the problem, differentiation was the solution. The district set out to change the performance curve by allocating different levels of resources to schools in the Red and Green Zones. In order to do this, Weast proposed a new way of thinking about equity: equity does not mean equal resources, it means equal opportunity. The reality is that unequal treatment is sometimes required to provide equal opportunity. In plain English, more money, more talent, and more time were essential if the Red Zone students could be expected to rapidly meet the same standards as Green Zone students. In the past, MCPS had allocated resources equally across all schools, regardless of need or performance. Even the funds coming from federal programs that focused on high-need students were stretched across the entire district. According to Weast, this method of resource allocation meant that the federal funds schools received were "not enough to really do anything meaningful."[2] In a series of community meetings in the fall of 1999, Weast explained the theory of unequal resource allocation, making the case that the Red Zone needed more time, better-trained teachers, and smaller class sizes to level the playing field. The annual per-pupil spending in MCPS in 1999 was around $11,000. Eventually, the Green Zone "subsidized" the Red Zone to the tune of $2,000 per student annually. There were no actual "transfer" payments between zones—Green Zone spending did not decrease to pay for increased Red Zone services—but the resource imbalance was real. Annual increases in Green Zone spending slowed significantly to permit new investments in the Red Zone, and Weast made no bones about it. Understandably, changing the current resource allocation system was met with some resistance and pushback from the community. As noted in chapter 1, a number of parents in wealthier parts of the county did not like the idea of moving resources from the more advantaged schools their children attended to low-performing schools. They were concerned that their children would be shortchanged in the process and that performance across the district would go down.

In part his message hinged on the doing the "right thing" for kids, but Weast also introduced the concept of a school district brand: good schools mean good neighborhoods, and good neighborhoods are good business. Not to put too fine a point on it, good schools are good for property values. Improving schools in less affluent neighborhoods would be good for the whole county. Building sufficient support from Green Zone parents allowed the district to invest heavily in Red Zone schools in an effort to accelerate the other part of its strategy, referred to as *push/pull*.

A PUSH/PULL APPROACH

Weast and his leadership team wanted performance to improve for kindergarten through grade 12, which Weast sometimes referred to as the entire *value chain*. They knew their efforts would be diluted in trying to attack every grade at once, so they decided to focus first on early-elementary literacy coupled with access to high school AP/honors courses. The two were strongly linked—the top readers in grade 3 eventually enrolled in the most rigorous classes in high school and went on to be successful in college and life. By focusing on the two ends of the value chain, the team hypothesized that a better-prepared cohort of elementary school graduates would *push* up into middle schools and force them to improve to meet their needs, while at the same time improved high schools would demand to *pull* better-prepared middle school graduates into their more rigorous environments. Hence the term *push/pull*. Weast explained the motivation for the approach, saying, "We knew that if we did this right, we could push the capacity for higher achievement, grade by grade, and shut down the argument that children would not be ready."[3]

With this in mind, Weast and his team centered the first wave of reforms in elementary schools. All of the district's 125 elementary schools would eventually participate in the strategy, but realizing that it could not do everything at once, the MCPS leadership team proposed to start in 60 focus schools in the Red Zone. These schools would create full-day kindergartens and reduce their class size in kindergarten through grade 2, and the district would provide teacher coaches in every building. The 60 focus schools served 75 percent of the elementary English as a Second Language (ESL) population, 80 percent of elementary students receiving free and reduced-price meals (FARMS), 78 percent of the total number of Hispanic students, and 70 percent of the elementary African American population. Called the Early Success Performance Plan, structural and curricular reforms at the focus schools were all aligned with the goal of improving grade 3 literacy.

To begin, full-day kindergarten was phased in at Red Zone elementary schools, with the highest-poverty schools converting first and with class sizes reduced to a student-to-teacher ratio of 15 to 1. MCPS revamped its kindergarten curricula and assessments, and established a benchmark for kindergarten reading that was much more rigorous than what had previously been expected of kindergarten students. Head Start programs were also brought into several Red Zone buildings, and their curriculum was aligned with the kindergartens', so that children as young as three and four entered the Pathway to Success. Investments in teacher knowledge and skill were critical to the conversion, a topic covered in depth in chapter 4. The results were a seamless early-childhood-to-elementary-school transition and students ready to learn when they walked into their first-grade classrooms on day one.

MCPS didn't stop at better preparing students for first grade. The class-size ratio for grades 1 and 2 was also reduced to a student-to-teacher ratio of 17 to 1, and specific reading interventions were implemented. Time for teaching reading was increased to ninety minutes, and students reading below grade level received an additional forty-five to sixty minutes of literacy instruction per day. Teachers, specialists, and other support personnel were also given professional development on literacy pedagogy for English language learners, special education students, and struggling readers.

On the other end of the continuum, it was long-standing policy that students required a teacher's recommendation to be considered for an AP or honors class; the team was dismayed to find that teachers often did not recommend qualified minority students for advanced courses. Weast envisioned a paradigm shift from a culture of competition, in which the highest-level courses have limited seats available only to an elite few, toward a new way of ensuring the success of every student through differentiated instruction, acceleration, and increased rigor. To break the barrier to honors and AP course enrollment, MCPS changed the policy and allowed students to choose whether or not they wanted to enroll in upper-level courses if they met certain criteria, such as minimum Preliminary SAT (PSAT) scores. This change, heralded by some as a move to equity and excellence for all students, was not entirely popular. Critics, including some parents of current AP and honors students, worried that the coursework would not be as challenging because teachers would have to water down the curriculum to accommodate less qualified students. This fear, however, has shown to be largely unfounded. Test scores for the types of students who have traditionally been enrolled in AP did not decline, even as many more minority students embraced the chance to take more difficult classes. This was a first step in changing the way teachers, students, and parents think about which students should participate in rigorous coursework.

UNCOVERING INCONSISTENCIES

As Weast and his team developed the district's overall strategy, it became clear that teachers and principals were using many different curricula with varying degrees of rigor. In the schools with the highest concentrations of poverty, MCPS teachers were using as many as fourteen different math textbooks. Instructional records were handwritten on three-by-five-inch cards, there was no centralized data source, and children who were moving around the district were changing textbooks and materials each time they moved. For children living in poor areas, whose families were highly mobile, the absence of standardized instruction presented an almost insurmountable obstacle to success.

During the strategy design phase, Weast met with the curriculum and instruction team to review the current guides and materials MCPS used. The day they met, the head of curriculum and instruction rolled a shopping cart into Weast's office; it was filled with heavy binders—the curriculum guides for just *one* content area. The guides were so heavy and unwieldy that teachers were not using them. It was no wonder that teaching varied widely, in content, rigor, and instruction. In the process, children were shortchanged, particularly those in low-income, high-mobility, and high-minority schools.

STARTING AT THE BEGINNING: THE KINDERGARTEN WARS

Having identified the lack of a core curriculum and acknowledged that reforms needed to begin at the elementary level, the executive team determined that MCPS needed to develop its own kindergarten curriculum. Together with the staged plan to move to a full-day kindergarten in the Red Zone, it was clear the curriculum had to be enlarged and augmented for the entire district. Because early-grade reading was correlated with so many later-grade benchmarks, the team believed that the curriculum had to be literacy based.

The curriculum development process grew out of the work of a planning committee that included representatives from the unions, parents, teachers, advocates, and curriculum writers from the district. There was enormous pressure—a mad dash—to create the curriculum so that it would be ready for rollout in fall 2000. Following stakeholder meetings in the spring, the group coalesced around four main ideas:

1. Young children have the ability to learn foundational skills, but they need to be taught explicitly.

2. The learning environment must be appropriate for five-year-olds.

3. Time must be used more efficiently.

4. Parents must play a role in supporting literacy skills at home.

The curriculum development committee used several MCPS sites that had solid programs—New Hampshire Estates, Bel Pre, and Rolling Terrace elementary schools—as models during the development phase. Using the Maryland State Department of Education's newly revised content standards, the committee outlined what children needed to be able to do in kindergarten in order to be on track for grade 3 and beyond.

The district provided an enormous amount of training to the teachers to help them adjust to the new curriculum. All kindergarten teachers were mandated to take one hundred hours of training over the summer; it was offered several times to accommodate the teachers' scheduling conflicts.

Initially, the idea of a rigorous kindergarten curriculum delivered in a full-day format generated pushback from both parents and teachers. In fact, MCPS veterans sometimes refer to that period as "the kindergarten wars." Some believed kindergarten should be purely developmental and students should not be taught to read if they were "not ready." Some felt that expectations for children were too high and students were going to be frustrated. Others felt the curriculum was too fast paced, but the district leadership team was committed to the reform. Dale Fulton, the associate superintendent for curriculum and instruction, oversaw the alignment of the curriculum. Having spent nearly thirty years in the MCPS, he understood the dramatic shift the kindergarten curriculum represented: "We weren't going to pay for mats anymore (for daytime naps). Kindergarten wasn't just going to be a place for kids to come and socialize. It was a place to come and build their skills and be prepared for more challenging curriculum."[4]

The idea of a systemwide curriculum with an assessment component was a new and challenging one to parents and teachers. The kindergarten reforms became a microcosm of the reform that would take place throughout the district. Teachers needed to be supported in ways that helped them accept that change was necessary and would be ultimately beneficial to everyone in the school system.

In fall 2000, MCPS implemented full-day kindergarten for the nineteen most severely impacted elementary schools in the Red Zone as a first step to implementing the reform districtwide. Because of the strategy's close association with the superintendent, these young students became known as "Jerry's kids" around the district. By midyear, some of the teachers were getting over the initial resistance to the new curriculum and assessment program. Many shared their surprise with each other and district leadership about what their children were able to do. Some admitted that they never would have believed it was possible. Remarkably, before the new curriculum was created, these students were only expected to read their names and identify some letters in the alphabet before rising to first grade.

To the surprise of several first-grade teachers in the fall semester of 2001, the majority of children from these schools arrived as accomplished readers. Before this, students from these highly impacted schools *learned* to read (if at all) in first grade. The pattern continued as full-day kindergarten spread throughout the Red Zone and then to the district as a whole—not only were kindergartners accelerating; students in each succeeding grade were reaching for more and getting more. By 2008, 93 percent of kindergartners were reading at or above standards, paving the way for higher achievement in middle school and eventually high school. "Jerry's kids" were on their way.

THINKING K–12

After the kindergarten curriculum was redesigned, the focus turned to math and other subject areas. Weast commissioned a curriculum audit—the first of its kind for the district. At Weast's request, in the summer of 2000, Phi Delta Kappa, a professional educators association, performed a K–12 math program audit and identified the weaknesses in the program and the areas of underperformance. Members of the team recalled this as a seminal moment leading to real transition. Auditors found that the curriculum and materials were not aligned internally nor were they aligned to state standards. And while the curriculum was adequate in scope, the quality was not good enough to aid teachers in differentiating their instruction to meet the various learning needs of their students. Materials were plentiful, but there was no systemwide focus or consistency.

The auditors also found substantial gaps in the level of success that African American, Hispanic, and FARMS students experienced. Given the degree of school-site and teacher autonomy in grouping students and selecting teaching materials, these findings did not come as a surprise.

Redesigning the math curriculum proved to be a difficult task. Prior to its revamping, the math instructional system was rigid, discrete, linear, and checklist oriented. This focus on basic math inhibited the move toward broad concepts and critical thinking.

People involved in the review process had widely divergent views about how the curriculum should be designed. One of their math textbook selections, *Everyday Mathematics*, had been publicly criticized by several notable professors from major universities. Some stakeholders felt the proposed curriculum was not rigorous enough and should concentrate more on computational skills. But MCPS's curriculum staff wanted a balanced approach to math, one that was conceptual yet skills based. There was considerable debate; at one point the MCPS staff participated in *Viewpoint*, a local call-in television program, where people asked questions about the reform. This helped to calm worries in the community and to build support for the vision of the county's curriculum staff.

The school board was fully supportive of the direction the curriculum department wanted to follow. To help to bolster its position, MCPS asked the College Board and Achieve Inc. to review its new math program. The College Board was the nonprofit responsible for administering the SAT and overseeing the AP curriculum and tests, while Achieve was an influential organization that helped define rigorous K–12 standards in math and English. Both groups approved the plan and gave it credibility.

With a general consensus behind it, MCPS directed all elementary schools to choose between two different math textbooks, *Harcourt* and *Everyday Mathematics*. By aligning the schools' math curricula to state standards, the administration hoped to have all students take Algebra 1 before entering ninth grade. The district's curriculum guides incorporated only these two textbook series, making it easier for the district to tailor teacher professional development programs to each school. The district also created a new position in high-poverty schools: math content coaches, who worked with teachers (kindergarten through grade 2) to help them refine their teaching skills. By sharing effective, research-based practices, they were able to help teachers use instructional strategies to reach all students.

The math audit process had measured the district's work against external quality standards, allowing leaders to gauge where they were versus where they wanted to be. It identified weaknesses in math that were applicable to other areas of the MCPS curriculum. MCPS had used the audit to overhaul its math curriculum, but saw some of the findings as applicable to all of the content areas:

- Variability in curriculum implementation

- Lack of curricular alignment

- Lack of curriculum-based diagnostic assessments

- Disparity among textbooks and materials used for instruction

- A gap in achievement between minority and nonminority students

- Lack of coherent, overall curriculum policy

INTEGRATE CURRICULUM, DIFFERENTIATE INSTRUCTION

Spurred by the results of the math audit, the board, with Weast's support, moved to address curriculum in a wholesale fashion, rather than piecemeal and subject by subject. Teams began to develop a common written curriculum across subjects that was aligned to standards, which all teachers would be expected teach. Working backward from rigorous high school AP standards, the teams would design the curriculum to ensure that no matter which school or classroom children attended, they would have access to a challenging, integrated curriculum. This was a revolutionary idea that challenged notions of educator autonomy as well as beliefs about what certain students were capable of learning.

The board curriculum policy called for a clear and coherent written curriculum aligned to standards. For each subject area, the board directed central office staff to develop a written framework and curriculum guides for each grade level and course. Developed by the MCPS Office of Instruction and Program Development (OIPD) in conjunction with the Council for Basic Education (CBE), the curriculum framework outlined the MCPS grades pre-K to 8 curricular goals, defined a vision of instruction and assessment, and provided precise expectations of what students were to know and be able to do by the end of each grade level or course in English/language arts, mathematics, science, and social studies.

Each of these elements was a part of the foundation necessary to create high-quality instruction. The frameworks provided raw material, and training gave teachers the skills to deliver the curriculum in ways that were tailored to the learning needs of their students. As curricula were developed, they were articulated at each level in terms of knowledge and skills. Assessments were created in both content and format.

Following the formal adoption of the comprehensive curriculum policy in February 2001, the district once again sought external review and validation of its curriculum as part of its cycle of continuous improvement. The district invited Achieve, along with the Council for

Basic Education and the College Board, to scrutinize the alignment of content standards, performance standards, and assessments. Overall, the Achieve report found that MCPS expectations were quite challenging and the semester final exams were well aligned to the state's content standards. On July 2, 2001, the board unanimously approved the MCPS curriculum framework.

CLARIFYING EXPECTATIONS

While the district was in the process of clearly defining student objectives, it also began to articulate expectations for teachers. In particular, the curriculum policy set a clear expectation that teachers would teach the "adopted" curriculum. This idea, that teachers had to teach a specific curriculum, was a striking change from what had been the norm. It challenged an existing notion of educator autonomy and deep assumptions about what certain students were capable of learning. Yet the notion that a common curriculum meant that all teachers were expected to teach the same way was inaccurate. Within the guidelines of the curriculum, teachers were expected to differentiate instruction based on the needs of their students. As a result, teachers not only had to be very familiar with the curriculum, but also had to understand what their students needed and what to do about it. Ensuring effective implementation required ongoing staff development, monitoring and supervision, periodic curriculum reviews, and frequent student assessment. Weast and his team believed these accountability mechanisms were absolutely necessary to prevent what they saw as one of their biggest challenges: a volunteer approach to implementation. While many teachers would enthusiastically engage in the new curriculum, there would be others who resisted by picking and choosing which pieces to use in their classroom. The review process would identify these teachers, and they would be counseled about the behavior to make certain that the curriculum was in place throughout the district.

In the primary grades, many teachers were distressed by the time it took to administer the new assessments that were required three to four times a year. But a key part of the strategy was that teachers would differentiate their delivery of the common curriculum based on their students' particular learning needs. In order to do this, they needed useful, frequent data about how their students were doing. Before this, there were no formal assessments, though some principals required their teachers to conduct informal observational reviews of their students' work. The new tests were administered one-on-one and required a good deal of time. They tested kindergarten students' knowledge in four main areas: letter knowledge, concepts about print, phonemic awareness, and a survey of oral language.

Responding to teacher concerns that the assessments were too long, and working closely with the union, the curriculum team made modifications to improve the curriculum implementation and assessments. To help teachers embrace and understand the new system, the district used outside consultants to facilitate ongoing training and to assist teachers in their classrooms during the transition. To make training more accessible, it was offered at different times to work with teachers' schedules. The training helped the teachers see themselves as active partners in the reform process rather than as recipients of another top-down directive. It also served as a job-fit screen for teachers, schools, and MCPS. As their questions were answered and concerns dealt with, teachers understood that the reforms were not voluntary. Most eventually embraced the reforms; however, some did not and left the school system.

As assessments revealed student gains, resistance to the changes diminished. Slowly, the concept evolved that staff development and teacher training was not about "fixing teachers" but about building skills to improve student outcomes.

INTEGRATING STANDARDS WHILE DIFFERENTIATING STRATEGY

One of the most significant ongoing challenges in MCPS has been implementing common grading and reporting standards. Without mechanisms to institutionalize the assumption that every child can reach high standards of learning, a new strategy predicated on resource and instructional differentiation was likely to produce the same result as previous reform efforts: predictable variability in outcomes.

When the MCPS team analyzed district grading policies, it found wide variability in expectations and procedures across the county. The problem was particularly jarring when team members examined the results of the end-of-course exam given to every algebra student in the district. A score of 66 was a D at the predominantly white Damascus High School, but was an A at Albert Einstein High School, where most students were minorities. Administrators were baffled. How could this happen? Even though the tests were the same countywide, individual schools and teachers were able to determine the grading criteria.

Minority parents were outraged when they learned that their children were not held to the same high standards as other students. Under the Red and Green Zone strategy, low-income and minority parents understood that their children would receive additional resources to bring them up to the *same levels* as white and affluent children. But if there were no common grading standards, how would the district ensure that this happened?

The school board and executive team attempted to instill uniform grading practices across MCPS in 2002 in the face of dramatic pushback from principals, teachers, and families. Implementation of the reformed grading policy was halted. Change on such an explosive issue would have to move more slowly.

The board and staff retooled and took a more collaborative approach with parents, teachers, and administrators. Weast formed a working group, made up of people throughout the community, whose mission was to make all grading systems consistent. The working group determined that grading and reporting was an important part of the larger effort to improve teaching and learning. The board and staff had always assumed this, but it was important for a broader group of stakeholders to work through the implications of the insight. The working group identified grading and reporting as important because it is an integral part of the instructional cycle—teachers communicate clear learning goals to students, plan instruction to meet those goals, give students feedback on their performance, offer students additional opportunities to learn, and collect evidence of student learning. It also should serve as an integrating mechanism for the district, as clear grading guidelines across a system help bring consistency of expectations.

In January 2004, the board approved a new five-year plan to implement a revised grading and reporting policy for MCPS, to begin in July 2004. The system was to provide meaningful standards-based feedback to students and parents. That same year, the district also published a step-by-step guide to help students and their families understand the expectations and preparation necessary for the most rigorous high school curriculum. Called Pathway to Success, the guide was communicated to every staff member and family in the district. At its most basic level, the Pathway to Success set forth seven steps to being college ready (see figure 2.1).

Despite substantial efforts, implementation of common grading and reporting continues to be a slow process. One analysis is that Weast

FIG. 2.1 **The Pathway to Success**

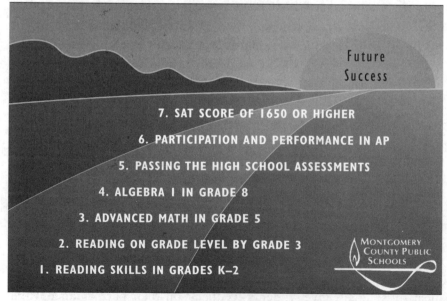

Future Success

7. SAT SCORE OF 1650 OR HIGHER

6. PARTICIPATION AND PERFORMANCE IN AP

5. PASSING THE HIGH SCHOOL ASSESSMENTS

4. ALGEBRA I IN GRADE 8

3. ADVANCED MATH IN GRADE 5

2. READING ON GRADE LEVEL BY GRADE 3

1. READING SKILLS IN GRADES K–2

MONTGOMERY COUNTY PUBLIC SCHOOLS

and his team initially underestimated the scope of the change they were asking of people. Practices—and the beliefs that supported them—diverged significantly from expectations. MCPS has found that staff, students, and parents needed time to understand the policy changes because the meaning of grades is intricately tied to belief systems. Many staff and parents consider grades to be rewards or punishments, and they use them to control student behavior. In some cases, they consider grading to be a win-lose proposition—one student can't win unless another student loses. The idea that all children can meet a standard is a concept that some people have difficulty accepting—if everyone can receive an A, then does the A lose its meaning?

Schools that developed a structured approach to implement the new policy fared well, while those that did not ensure staff understanding and commitment found themselves surrounded by anxious students and parents. In any reform, lasting success depends on commitment rather than compliance. Changes to grading and reporting have not been met with open arms because not all parents, students, and school staff have fully embraced the beliefs embedded in the effort. Unlike with curricular and grade-level reforms, MCPS tried to implement these changes all at once, not phased in over time, causing some teachers to initially comply with the new system without being fully committed to the change process. Over time, they reverted to their default assumptions and expectations.

In 2005, the executive leadership team again slowed the process down, to continue the work steadily to generate consensus. The team created systemwide ownership of the initiative—policy decisions driven by the board of education that involve the input of deputy and associate superintendents, the director of curriculum and instruction, and multistakeholder committees consisting of union presidents, parents, students, teachers, and business and community leaders.

In 2006, MCPS began its third year of implementation of the revised grading and reporting policy by field-testing standards-based electronic report cards and a Web-based grading and reporting system for grades 1 and 2. This reform process is ongoing and continues to involve many people throughout the community. Sustained outreach programs—mailings, handouts, videos, and brochures, among others—and efforts to build consensus all help to transmit the district's message and communicate the need for the full implementation of the common standards.

BOOKENDING REFORM

Extending reform to high school has also been a challenge. The work began after the 2000 audit, but implementation has been difficult. Aligning the curriculum and assessments with standards across a range of subjects required numerous iterations. Consequently, MCPS focused its initial high school efforts on AP and honors course enrollment—completion of these types of classes demonstrated college readiness. The first step was to identify an external measure of readiness for such courses. Looking at the research, MCPS found that the PSAT exam could serve as a screening tool for unidentified high-potential students. In fact, the district found that the PSAT was a good predictor of student success in honors and AP courses; nearly two-thirds of MCPS AP test takers with PSAT verbal scores of 42 to 46 or math scores of 43 to 47 earned scores of 3 or higher on English, math, science, and social studies AP exams.

Taking these findings into account, the MCPS Department of Shared Accountability analyzed eleventh-grade students' PSAT scores and honors and AP course enrollment. All the students who were not enrolled in any honors or AP courses but scored a 44 or above on the PSAT math or verbal sections were identified. As Weast said, "We broke that barrier in high school by opening up courses to student choice and using the PSAT to identify students who would have been overlooked, many of them African American and Hispanic."[5]

Principals then received two lists consisting of these students—one with all the students' names and another with just the Hispanic and African American students. The understanding was that principals and counselors would work together to enroll students on the second list in honors and AP courses. But there was still resistance. Some argued that the students weren't prepared, they didn't have high enough grades, or the classes were already at capacity. While the early-elementary re-forms were well on their way, increasing rigor for all students at the high school level would move at a slower pace. We will come back to this later in our story.

REFLECTIONS ON THE JOURNEY

Each element of the strategy created disequilibrium in the community when it was implemented. For instance, the differentiated approach was often greeted with a measure of distrust and suspicion, a reaction voiced by both teachers and parents. During the kindergarten cur-riculum rollout, Weast often dropped in on teacher training sessions and took questions. During one of these visits, a teacher from a Green Zone school that would not have the Red Zone's smaller class sizes pointedly asked Weast how she was supposed to do all of this with twenty-five students in her classroom. He paused for a moment and then asked her whether she would like to move over to one of the Red Zone schools where she could have a class of fifteen. The room was silent as people grappled with the fact that there were different needs in differ-ent parts of the county, and they would all be dealt with differently.

Yet Weast knew that to convince teachers that he wanted to help them, he could not simply tell them that what they were doing was wrong; instead, he worked closely with the teachers union, trying to gain their trust and to include them in every aspect of both the reform details and the implementation process. We will discuss this in chapter 3.

Darlene Merry, associate superintendent of organizational develop-ment, had many meetings with principals and district administrators during the implementation phase. She had spent more than twenty years as a teacher and principal in the district before taking a cen-tral office role, and she had deep relationships with teachers around MCPS. She recalled, "We had lots of tough meetings when pursuing these reforms. We had imposed a different level of accountability at the school level, and there was definitely a feeling that the stakes were higher. So it was very important that we listened to their concerns and gained their trust."[6]

In addition to pushback from staff, others in the community were also skeptical about the reforms in the early days. Some parents in high-performing schools were fearful their children would be "missing out" if financial resources were distributed based on need. Over time, however, as the minority achievement gap narrowed and test scores across the district rose, there was more widespread support for the changes. Early improvements in student literacy demonstrated the strategy's effectiveness to the community and enabled its expansion to grades 1–2, then to grades 3–5. Each year, the community saw substantial gains in student achievement, which validated the effectiveness of a focus on literacy, an emphasis on math, and access to rigorous high school courses. Eventually, most community members came to understand the power of a strategy based not on equal resources, but on equal opportunity.

CONCLUSION

Through a series of systematic reforms that evolved over the first several years of Weast's tenure, the school district began to address the problems that had plagued it for decades. It began with a clear theory—a differentiated approach to allocating financial and human resources combined with a deliberate strategy to differentiate the delivery of a rigorous integrated curriculum. The Red and Green Zones provided a framework for sequencing initiatives, beginning with instructional and structural reforms at the early-elementary and high school levels, followed by systemwide curricular audits. As Weast describes it, "The most important thing we did was focus on differentiation, beginning with instruction. It is how you approach individual students . . . This is the basis of our organizational strategy. Differentiating what a school needs or a teacher needs based upon what a kid needs has been critical to our progress."[7]

MCPS created a new social compact in which those with more assets had the wisdom to see that their interests could be served by investing in less affluent areas of the community in order to raise the opportunity for everyone. Green Zone constituents were eventually convinced that the district would continue to push their children for excellence, even as a differentiation strategy was deployed in the Red Zone. MCPS was able to maintain the good will of the Green Zone while investing heavily in the Red Zone partly because of Weast's political and rhetorical skills and his moral vision, but also because of the hard work of teachers and principals around the district—as Red Zone schools produced results and Green Zone schools remained excellent, parents and other stakeholders were more willing to support the strategy. When community members of different economic classes were given a compelling reason to strengthen the whole community, they demonstrated what is best about America: individual interests and the common good can be pursued in tandem. By making school reform everyone's problem—and everyone's opportunity—and aligning teachers, curriculum, and systems to reach the common goal, the district was able to begin the process of transformation. Even so, sustaining momentum as a strategy progresses is difficult and requires deep and broad support from multiple constituencies. How did various stakeholders come together to support continuous improvement? We will explore this question in chapter 3.

CHAPTER THREE

Building Relationships for Sustainability

Weast had an iconoclastic view of how to engage groups that often act as barriers to improvement; . . . a "system of shared accountability" . . . would encompass the employee unions, the school board, and the county council, as well as district and school staff and parents.

Critical to any reform effort is building supporting coalitions. Without support from key stakeholders, change efforts sputter and eventually fail. For Weast and his team, the need for building support among stakeholders was even higher. MCPS had proposed a controversial strategy in *Our Call to Action*—one that placed equity of opportunity, not equality of resources, above everything else. They were able to create momentum for the need to change and develop broad agreement about their North Star and the strategy of differentiation that would get them there, but the hardest work remained. Everyone—parents, teachers, principals, support staff, board members, union leaders, politicians, government officials, civic and community representatives, business leaders, and students themselves—would have to find ways to support the strategy for creating excellence and equity for every child in MCPS.

Brokering agreements with every stakeholder group is a fine goal, but sometimes it can seem impractical. An alternative approach is to assess which mix of relationships—or coalitions—might provide a counterweight to factions that could attempt to block key elements of a strategy over time. In chapter 1, we described how Weast spent his first few months deeply engaged in the community during the development and communication of *Our Call to Action*. That process provided him with an opportunity to assess the operating style of each of these groups, as well as their capacity for engaging productively in the reform. On the basis of this analysis, he began a process of pushing groups to increase their effectiveness while at the same time using his political skills to find ways to build connections among these groups in ways that would support his agenda for breaking the link between race, income, and student outcomes.

Our Call to Action became a compact between the school and the community, creating a shared sense of purpose and responsibility. It called upon everyone to play a part in school reform, and it provided information and markers of success in an easy-to-read, accessible format. Weast had an iconoclastic view of how to engage groups that often act as barriers to improvement in large districts—he believed in blurring the lines between governance and management to create a "system of shared accountability" that would encompass the employee unions, the school board, and the county council, as well as district and school staff and parents. If he could engage these groups in collaborative problem analysis, strategy design, and implementation planning, not only would the strategy be more powerful because of their input, but they would feel more invested in supporting it over the long term.

PARTNERING WITH THE UNIONS

Ask some district veterans what the biggest factor in MCPS's success has been, and they will reply with one word: *unions*. What they really mean is that the commitments that the three bargaining units in Montgomery County made to improve the capacity of their members to deliver results for students were an invaluable accelerant to the improvement strategy. The three unions—Montgomery County

Education Association (MCEA) for teachers, Montgomery County Association of Administrative and Supervisory Personnel (MCAASP) for administrators, and the Service Employees International Union (SEIU) Local 500 for support staff—played a vital role in the development, implementation, and modification of MCPS's strategy. And Weast not only encouraged their engagement; in some cases, he insisted on it. The relationship he built with Mark Simon and Bonnie Cullison of MCEA, Ed Shirley and Rebecca Newman of MCAASP, Merle Cuttitta of SEIU, and other union leaders has allowed for disagreements on particular issues without derailing the objectives they share for student learning. Rather than all sides positioning themselves primarily as adversaries, they generally behave as partners. Together, they created a breakthrough working collaboration with a focus on meeting the district's goals for student performance.

The groundwork for a productive relationship had been laid prior to Weast's arrival. In the mid-1990s, the unions began collaborating on issues that were beneficial to all three groups. Most importantly, the leadership of the unions joined with the district to implement interest-based bargaining when each was negotiating its respective contract. Described in Fisher and Ury's classic, *Getting to Yes*, interest-based bargaining was in contrast to the traditional positional bargaining process that many districts and unions undertake, where parties anchor at extreme positions and take hard stands, in the hope that the ultimate settlement will be favorable.[1] Instead, the unions and MCPS committed to a process where the focus is on actual needs rather than stated positions. They separated the people from the issues, generated multiple options before making decisions, and defined successful outcomes on objective standards. Yet, at the time, the relationship between MCPS and the unions was somewhat strained. The district was operating under an environment of limited financial resources and had to end each budgeting process by making "nonrecommended" cuts. Positions were lost and benefits curtailed. The situation was exacerbated as MCPS negotiated unequal percentage pay increases for each employee group during contract negotiations.

The arrival of Weast took the district–unions relationship to a new level. First, he and chief operating officer Larry Bowers reaffirmed MCPS's commitment to interest-based bargaining. Bowers had spent more than twenty years in MCPS, including time as a deputy superintendent and chief financial officer, and had seen more confrontational approaches to the union fail to produce results. He and Weast also supported equity in the negotiated agreements for each of the unions and continue to do so today. Pay increases for the three unions have been relatively equal since 2000. Bowers and Weast also did something that is impossible to imagine from most superintendents. They proposed that the unions and their members be actively engaged in the district's work. More recently, union presidents have become full members of the executive leadership team that included all of the deputy superintendents, associate superintendents, and other top leaders who reported to Weast, and they and their staffs serve on the operations and capital budget committees. MCPS's emphasis on treating each employee group equally, dedication to interest-based negotiations, and ardor for blurring the lines brought a new level of collaboration to the system—one where teachers, administrators, and support staff could talk about and work toward solving common problems.

Since then, the returns on MCPS's investments in its relationship with the unions have been extraordinary. In collaboration with MCEA president Bonnie Cullison, Weast and Bowers have been able to implement numerous groundbreaking reforms that have changed the role and career path of teachers in MCPS. Cullison, a longtime fourth- and fifth-grade teacher and speech pathologist prior to being elected president of the union, saw the collaboration with Bowers and Weast as a way to increase the professionalism of teaching. Together, they developed the comprehensive Professional Growth System (PGS), which included a model Peer Assistance and Review (PAR) program and the career lattice, a leadership pathway for teachers, all of which are discussed in greater detail in chapter 4. MCAASP president Rebecca Newman, Cullison, and Bowers also negotiated an administrator–teacher collaboration period in the school day to meet, plan, and assess the effectiveness of their instructional approaches. Providing teachers and principals with the time necessary for data-driven inquiry and planning fostered a deeper commitment to reform.

Engaging MCAASP with the same depth as with MCEA took more time. Because of its relatively small membership and budget, MCAASP had no resources to pay its president in the early days of Weast's tenure. He worked as a high school principal in the district, so when there was an advisory group or committee meeting during the working day, he had to take leave to attend, unlike the other two union presidents, who were devoted full-time to union work. Weast wanted the president to be a full participant and, with Bowers' help, brokered an agreement in which MCAASP agreed to have its members contribute one day of personal leave each year to pay for the president's salary. This allowed the president to devote full time to his union role and to participate more fully in the districtwide leadership activities. The effort paid off. Currently, under Newman's leadership, principal representatives have joined more than thirty project teams and work groups, and each deputy and associate superintendent has a principals' advisory group made up of twelve to fifteen principals who have regular opportunities to provide input to the work of these departments.

Members of a school district's support staff—bus drivers, lunch servers, secretaries, and others—often feel disengaged from the process of educating children. They are not included in major decisions and by and large feel voiceless in the system. Not in MCPS. Weast, Bowers, and the president of SEIU Local 500, Merle Cuttitta, worked to ensure that everyone knew how essential support staff was to improving student achievement. Cuttitta had been a paraeducator and administrative assistant in MCPS before winning the presidency of Local 500, which had jurisdiction of all private and public sector SEIU members in Maryland and Washington, D.C. As part of this new outreach, employees such as bus drivers and lunchroom staff were told how important they were to student success, and, more significantly, were given as much respect as teachers, principals, and top administrators. Teachers union president Cullison explained, "A lot of districts ignore the role and responsibility of every staff member in the system and that is where it breaks down. If you don't have a building operating in a way that facilitates learning, it won't happen. Bus drivers, para-educators, and lunch room staff are all critical in creating the environment for the instructional core. It is an integrated system and everything counts. If you don't pay attention to one part, it will sabotage your work."[2]

The multiparty relationship was valuable in negotiations between any of the employee groups and the district, but it was also useful when disputes arose between the members of each group. For instance, nearly all teachers and most support staff reported to a principal, and sometimes grievances occurred that rose to the level of union leadership. Because the three unions had developed horizontal relationships with each other, these issues were sometimes easier to resolve. At times the unions stepped up to help keep the districtwide strategy moving forward. For example, in a tough budget environment in the 2003–2004 school year, the unions agreed to defer $14 million in wage increases in order to preserve investments in the Red Zone.

By 2005, MCPS, MCEA, MCAASP, and SEIU Local 500 had co-created and signed a formal plan of collaboration and respect. The "culture of respect" compact, painstakingly developed by the three unions and MCPS senior staff, recognizes that all MCPS employees have valuable roles they play in the learning community. The document was later incorporated as an addendum to the district's strategic plan, to signify its importance. It emphasizes seven key points that spell out the acronym RESPECT:

- Resolving differences
- Enhancing collaboration
- Supporting coworkers
- Promoting civility
- Encouraging creativity

- Communicating openly

- Team building through trust

The compact reinforces the culture of teamwork and shared accountability that all parties are working to create. It is a powerful lever in the strategy to break the link between race, class, and student performance.

INVOLVING THE SCHOOL BOARD AND COUNTY COUNCIL

We all know just how "political" public education can be. Public education is the stage on which a community's hopes, fears, and expectations play out, from conventional questions about standards and grades to more controversial matters like sex education, bilingual education, and racial integration. The politics of education extend two-dimensionally, into the organization itself and outside the organization. Just as it is essential for the superintendent to gain the confidence of the faculty and staff, he or she must gain the confidence of the voters. As Weast says, "We're in the marketplace of ideas and results, and the community must have confidence in what we say and do."[3] In MCPS, success or failure to do so plays out in two places: the Montgomery County Board of Education (the board) and the Montgomery County Council (the council). In addition, voters elect a county executive, who functions basically as a county mayor. The executive serves the traditional executive branch function and is critical in the budget process.

The relationship between MCPS, the board, and the council is complex. The board consists of seven county residents elected by voters for four-year terms and a student elected by secondary school students for a one-year term. They form the official policy-making body for MCPS and are responsible for selecting the superintendent. Separately, the council is made up of nine members who are elected to serve concurrent four-year terms. The council sets the local property tax rate, and while MCPS and the board work to develop the budget for each school year, it is the council that approves the budget (or not) and provides the majority of the money—approximately 75 percent of the overall budget. Once MCPS develops its budget, it is sent to the executive, who folds it into his overall county budget before submitting it to the council. County executive Doug Duncan, whose tenure started several years prior to Weast's, became a strong supporter of the system's reforms after being somewhat skeptical at first. Nearly every year, he had recommended that the system receive nearly 100 percent of its budget request.

A budget is simply a dollars-and-cents expression of an organization's purpose and procedures. The more transparent and open the budget-building process is—and the more transparent the budget itself is—the greater the likelihood that the funding body will approve it. There was great skepticism at the council level about the school system's reforms and whether they would work. Weast built an early relationship with council education committee chair Michael Subin, a council veteran with a forceful and determined personality. In addition, Weast cultivated relationships with the other council members, including Steve Silverman, who ultimately became a champion of the system's work and its effort to reduce class size. Because of the strong relationships, the results the system was able to show, and the community support, the council approved budget increases of $100 million a year for six years. How was this accomplished? The story begins with trust and respect, but it can only continue with demonstrable results. Weast began working to build these conditions in his first months as superintendent.

In 1999, board members had frosty relationships with one another and basically agreed on only one thing: they were looking for a leader to replace outgoing superintendent Paul Vance, an African American who initiated the first districtwide academic reforms under the Success for Every Student plan. The board wanted a dynamic person committed to taking those reforms and raising student achievement well beyond current expectations. They interviewed more than ten candidates and finally settled on one; to their dismay, they learned that the candidate had withheld personal financial information that had become public and problematic. The board, up against a tight deadline, went back to square one. Because of state requirements, if it didn't hire a new superintendent by July 15, it would not be able to appoint a permanent superintendent until the following year.

Weast was headed for vacation when he was approached by the board. He had not applied for the position and told the board when he agreed to an interview that he wasn't completely committed to taking the position if offered. After speaking with members, Weast believed that the board had sufficient commitment to raising the bar and closing the gap and that the county had the financial resources to do it. Within ten days, the board was unanimous in its desire to hire Weast but had more difficulty in developing consensus around the details of his contract. Some members didn't want to pay him more than the previous superintendent, and others thought he hadn't sufficiently proved himself, since his previous district had only sixty thousand students. Some stakeholders who had the ear of particular board members expressed concern that his academic credentials had been conferred by state universities in the Midwest rather than elite East Coast institutions. In the end, the board voted four to three to approve the contract provisions required to bring Weast to Montgomery County.

Upon his arrival, Weast immediately worked to build relationships with board members by meeting with each individually. After a seven-week whirlwind of data gathering, meetings, and learning about the culture, structures, and processes of MCPS, Weast was prepared to present what he had learned to the board at a three-day retreat. Even though he had not received unanimous support for his contract, he wanted to unify the members and get their full support for the plan that he would present to them in less than seven weeks and for the budget he would present to them one month later.

His goal for the retreat was to get the board to set its priorities for the school system and to commit to these priorities, because Weast intended to use these priorities to develop his plan of action. This was a lofty goal for a new superintendent and quite a challenge since the board often did not reach consensus on much of anything. The only attendees at the meeting were board members and their staff, Weast, his executive assistant, and two deputy superintendents. They agreed to hire a facilitator to try to bring the board together. At one point, things were so strained that the facilitator had members use laptop computers to communicate with each other to dissipate some of the tension.

During the retreat, Weast presented the board with extensive data about the school system. He did not try to cover up any of the problems. A significant performance gap existed between white and Asian American students and their Hispanic and African American peers, and the current performance could not be sustained because of the dramatically changing demographics. After much discussion and debate, the board agreed on a list of priorities, and approved them several days later at a separate meeting. These priorities guided the work of Weast's staff over the next seven weeks as they developed *Our Call to Action*. This original set of priorities has guided the work of the district since then and has only been changed twice in nine years. As board member Patricia O'Neill said, "We pledged at that retreat that we weren't going to throw rocks at each other or do anything to take up staff time that would take us away from the priorities. We all rose to the occasion and became bigger people. We have done a pretty good job of sticking to the plan and not becoming road blocks."[4]

Weast's leadership and honesty earned the board's trust, but there were still the executive and the council to convince. Armed with a comprehensive strategy set forth in *Our Call to Action*, the executive and the council decided to go along with the plan and supported MCPS's budget with an additional $100 million that first year. As for the next five years of budget increases, Weast and his team had to show the board and the council proof that the plan was working, and that he did. Each year, Weast revisited the goals and outcomes set forth in *Our Call to Action*. He showed what happened in the previous year and the adjustments that were made to increase effectiveness. The board and the council saw that their support and money were improving student achievement for all students in Montgomery County. It was the start of what Weast came to call "the virtuous cycle." Results bring more resources, which allow you to build more capacity to produce better results, starting the cycle anew.

CONNECTING WITH PARENTS

MCPS made a concerted effort to bring parents into the reform equation as full partners. This was a significant change from previous administrations and helped to shore up community support. Many parents feel alienated from their schools, particularly low-income and nonnative English speakers. They are intimidated by the school system, unwilling or unable to speak to the teachers, and are uncertain about how to help their children succeed academically and socially. From the beginning, Weast reached out to these disenfranchised parents, turning to his communications team, led by Aggie Alvez, to develop a comprehensive outreach strategy. Alvez, a former social studies teacher and the district's human relations compliance officer, understood the challenges of communicating effectively with families from diverse backgrounds. During the fall of 2000, Weast and his team conducted sixteen forums throughout the county, including four for multicultural communities, requiring interpreting services in Spanish, Chinese, Korean, Japanese, and Vietnamese. Parents were invited to be part of smaller working groups to discuss all aspects of school reform, including curriculum changes and budgeting decisions. Then Weast and his team did something potentially more important—they listened carefully and incorporated many of the suggestions into the strategy. Parents could see the result of their interaction with the district in the final version of *Our Call to Action*.

This signaled that the district wanted the lines of communication to run both ways. MCPS continued to bolster its relationship with parents by making as much information as possible clear and accessible. All materials related to school improvements and reforms were made public, both in hard copy and online, and published in multiple languages—Chinese, French, Korean, Spanish, and Vietnamese.

Critical to the success of MCPS's new strategy was the support of parents in the Green Zone. The message that resources were being targeted in Red Zone schools had the potential to be misinterpreted and could sabotage MCPS's entire strategy. Weast and his team knew it was important not to become embroiled in a fight with parents that nobody would win. They had to stay above the fray and clearly communicate that the strategy made sense for everybody because all students would benefit. As Weast said, "Staying on message was critical. And because there was a well-crafted communications plan, people were able to reiterate the message, and it wasn't just something that you read or saw. The message had been internalized so well that we had leaders in the community coming forward to support these efforts."[5]

In recent years, MCPS has worked hard to make parent involvement standard operating procedure for everything it does. A districtwide Parent Advisory Council was created, and feedback has been systematically collected in six different languages on every major issue impacting MCPS. Alvez and her team developed nontraditional ways to reach out to underrepresented parent groups. They created television programs and videos for those parents who were not literate in their own language. The district also made it possible for parents to go online to review their children's assignments and grades and to communicate with teachers. Parents can track their children's progress and then discuss with their children their performance in a particular area. Parents who have a question can e-mail teachers and get an immediate response.

Making information available—district strategy, standards, school success measures, student achievement across the board, and the achievement of their own children in particular—put parents in the driver's seat. Knowledge is power, and when parents have information about the district's responsibilities and expectations, for itself and for all students, they feel more invested in the reform process. Weast built on parents' engagement by inviting them to be a part of the process through committees that were organized to craft various interventions and implementation plans related to the strategy. This gave parents an ownership stake in MCPS's successes *and* its challenges, which gave Weast and his team the support and the time they needed to implement their controversial strategy of differentiated resources and instruction.

ENGAGING THE BUSINESS COMMUNITY

The Montgomery County business community has been an important supporter of the district's improvement. Businesses can be critical partners in the coalition to raise student achievement and close the achievement gap, but their efforts must be more strategic than "principal for a day" or "adopt a school" programs. In particular, forging meaningful relationships with business leaders to assist in expanding and developing the knowledge and skills of people in the organization can be powerful. A strategic relationship with business taps into more than altruism, though that is important. Businesses also have a vested interest in the quality of the community's schools. They hire graduates, and their employees send their children to the local schools. Healthy local economies are good for business, and high-quality schools are an important part of this.

Businesses in Montgomery County are becoming involved in schools in new ways. They are helping to identify the skills and knowledge that students need for success and are forming executive-level partnerships with senior staff in MCPS. The biggest driver of these activities has been the Montgomery County Business Roundtable for Education (MCBRE). The nonprofit organization works closely with MCPS to help find innovative approaches to school improvement and to offer lessons from business as the senior team grapples with building capacity in the district.

MCBRE's mission is to "connect classroom learning to the workplace." In its early years, MCBRE supported a number of disconnected programs; some dealt with immigrant housing, while others focused on adult literacy. More recently, it strengthened its partnership with MCPS through deeper engagements with students and by creating a joint platform for cross-sector knowledge sharing.

MCBRE's student-centered initiatives include "720," a program where up-and-coming business leaders address the entire ninth-grade class about the importance of the next 720 days of high school; and Emerging Student Leaders, a selective leadership program where black and Hispanic students attend the Congressional Black Caucus (CBC) Foundation and Congressional Hispanic Caucus (CHC) Institute. Attendees then develop personal advocacy projects, which are presented at the end of the year. Noted one student who participated in the 2005 program, "Before CBC, I thought about things on a much smaller scale, focusing much of my attention on my own local community. After I attended the program, I saw how expansive the issues in our country are . . . I've become more involved on a larger level—national, state—and local as well . . . I now see the bigger picture. I've come to the realization that we don't necessarily live in a bubble and perhaps by working with a more diverse set of peers—location, age, gender, race—we can speed up the process of solving the problems we face today."[6]

While programs such as 720 and Emerging Student Leaders allowed a direct student–business connection, MCBRE has influenced the entire system through such knowledge-sharing projects as Operational Excellence and board of advisers meetings. Operational Excellence, or OpEx, began as a five-month-long collaboration between thirteen public school system leaders and twenty-five business leaders. The purpose was to find ways the school system could use best practices to improve productivity in some of its business practices. Many recommendations from this business–education partnership have been implemented, and as a result MCPS has been able to increase operating efficiencies and achieve substantial cost savings. Taking OpEx a step further, MCBRE, under the leadership of then-president Jane Kubasik, started to hold regular board of advisers meetings. At the sessions, executives from the top businesses in Montgomery County, such as Deloitte, PricewaterhouseCoopers, and UnitedHealthcare, engage with top leaders from MCPS. Experts in innovation, change management, employee engagement, managing multigenerational differences, and other germane topics address the gathering, and then the business and education leaders share with each other their relevant experience and thoughts on the day's topic. Some of the sessions are designed to produce action items for the district. For instance, one board of advisers meeting led to MCPS setting the benchmark that 80 percent of its students would be college ready by 2014.

EXTENDING CAPACITY THROUGH PARTNERSHIPS

Large urban school districts are inundated with requests from local and national organizations to form partnerships. For Weast and his team, the challenge was forming deep partnerships with a select few that reinforced MCPS's overall strategy. Consequently, MCPS decided to collaborate closely with colleges and universities, Ruth Rales Comcast Kids Reading Network, and African American and Hispanic advocacy organizations.

MCPS, Montgomery College, and the University System of Maryland have a joint interest in producing citizens who have the interpersonal and intellectual skills to be competitive in a global economy. They share the belief that all students matter and are entitled to the opportunity to access rigorous educational opportunities. Each institution is committed to innovative projects designed to raise the level of student achievement and overall academic performance. The expectations for educational excellence in Montgomery County require expansive pathways to postsecondary education. College coursework at the high school level is a vehicle to expand of the students' intellectual capital. Allowing high school students to experience the challenge of college-level courses while providing opportunities to earn college credit is a critical component in a comprehensive effort to prepare students for postsecondary study and work. To this end, the partners work collaboratively to develop successful pathways to college and career readiness for every MCPS student.

This partnership provides dual enrollment opportunities and offers a broad spectrum of opportunities for students and staff through a variety of programs. The Gateway to College program is targeted to MCPS students between the ages of sixteen and twenty who are not succeeding in high school and either have stopped attending or are not on track to earn a high school diploma. The program offers students the chance to continue high school coursework while earning college credits at Montgomery College. Students also receive personal counseling and guidance, assistance with problem solving, and time and stress management. The program provides students at risk of not graduating with the opportunity to earn their high school diploma while transitioning to a college campus.

The Ruth Rales Comcast Kids Reading Network—a joint project of MCPS, the RFI Foundation, Comcast, and the Montgomery County government—provides weekly tutoring to second-grade students who are at risk for reading proficiency. Over 750 second-grade students in 70 elementary schools benefit from weekly tutoring by a trained volunteer. On average, students gain at least one grade level in reading fluency and comprehension by the end of the program. Volunteers are senior citizens, working adults, parents, grandparents, and students. The program's success is due in part to the high quality of the materials and the training provided to the tutors. One volunteer shared, "When I first met my student, I was nervous. I said, 'We're going to have to do a partnership here. We will read books together. I will help you and you will help me; because there may be some words that I don't know.' I now look forward to going to the school every week and working with Tyler. We read and talk about what we have read. Tyler recently told me that, because of me, he has read more books in the past couple of months than he had read in his whole life. His reading skills have improved and he feels good about himself."[7]

MCPS works to involve Hispanic and African American members of the community in the strategy. The district works closely with the National Association for the Advancement of Colored People (NAACP), Identity (a Latino youth organization), Upcounty and Downcounty Latino Network, Montgomery County Latino Education Coalition, and other advocacy organizations. Representatives from these organizations and others played a key role in the development of MCPS's strategic plan and continue to serve on systemwide work groups and advisory committees. They also meet monthly with the deputy superintendent, Frieda Lacey, as a part of her Deputy's Minority Achievement Advisory Committee.

CONCLUSION

The broad-based leadership that emerged from the unions, the board, and the council was critical to the early momentum of the differentiation strategy and has been a consistent force for improvement throughout the nearly ten-year journey. Some superintendents might have seen the divisions between board members and among the three labor organizations as an opportunity to consolidate power by exploiting those tensions. Instead, Weast chose in effect to mediate these disagreements so that each of the groups would function more productively in their own work and would be better partners for the district in implementing the strategy. Make no mistake—the credit for the important roles they have played in improving student learning goes to their leaders and members, but in those first months of his superintendency, Weast made a strategic choice to invest himself in building relationships with these bodies even as he helped them build their capacity.

Of particular note is the consistency of the support from the board and the council, even as their memberships have changed over time. Of the members in place when Weast was hired, only one from the board and one from the council are still in place, yet the bodies both support *Our Call to Action* as strongly as the groups that voted for it in the beginning. This kind of support over several election cycles, even as members were coming and going, has been critical to Weast's tenure, which at ten years is longer than that of the average large district superintendent by about three times over.

The proactive approach to building partnerships with parents, businesses, and community partners is also an instructive model of how to think of these relationships as "accelerants" for the strategy, as Weast calls them. In each instance, with parents, MCBRE, and the universities and community groups, the partnerships are designed to add capacity for the work the district is trying to accomplish. For each of them, you can draw a clear line from the collaborative activity to some element of the strategy, whether it is early-grade reading, high school success, or accelerated performance for African American and

Hispanic students. As obvious as it seems, most districts have great difficulty managing their stakeholder relationships in ways that focus them more intensely on implementing their strategy.

While partnerships with key stakeholders have extended the district's capacity, the real engine for performance is the teachers, school leaders, support staff, and central office teams that are ultimately responsible for the students in Montgomery County. In chapter 4, we will explore MCPS's approach to investing in its most important accelerant: its people.

CHAPTER FOUR

Expanding Capacity Through Investments in People

Once a district has a viable strategy, it faces two central capacity-building challenges. The first is delivering excellence when the scale is vast ...The second is speed. The capacity of its people must be built at an accelerating pace over time to keep up with the momentum and expectations created by early wins.

At the core of MCPS's strategy is the belief that a great teacher in every classroom is the foundation for student success. Among other things, teachers in Montgomery County must know how to work together to understand the learning needs of their students and deliver a rigorous curriculum in differentiated ways to meet those needs. The district was willing to invest heavily in helping teachers gain the knowledge and skills they needed to understand the curriculum, diagnose student needs, and adjust their instructional practice to help students meet standards. MCPS also understood that people in a variety of leadership and support roles needed to increase their capacity to strengthen and support the work of teachers in classrooms. Principals needed ongoing training in instructional leadership and change management; teachers in leadership roles and on special assignments needed to acquire coaching and collaborative skills to extend their instructional expertise to their colleagues; and school-based teams needed help in working together as problem solvers. The challenge was enormous, but if the differentiation strategy were to be successful, the skill and knowledge of nearly everyone in the district would need to rapidly and continuously improve.

The concept of professional development, or PD, is not new to education; in fact, it is often seen as a panacea—as someone has described it, "The sector worships at the altar of PD." Unfortunately, measurable results in student learning rarely materialize after significant professional development investments. The MCPS team was well aware of this fact and worked to avoid the biggest pitfall of PD spending: expensive, episodic training events about the latest theory or fad without a clear link to the knowledge and skills required by an explicit improvement strategy. Instead, they designed a comprehensive people investment approach that was tied directly to the district's overall strategy of raising the bar and closing the gap through differentiated instruction of a rigorous common curriculum.

The original statements about the importance of investments in people in 1999's *Our Call to Action* served as a guide:

> As policy makers, we cannot mandate what matters. We must rely on local capacity and local will. Our instructional staff—teachers, support staff and administrators—must be helped to develop the capability [to] act in new ways, and they must be willing to own the changes needed. We must reorganize our resources to meet their needs in the classroom.
>
> The quality of teaching makes the difference, and our resources should be focused on all efforts to support teaching and learning. The workforce should receive the resources to strengthen itself and must integrate research and practice, engage in shared inquiry, examine itself and experiment with new approaches.[1]

Even in the best political and financial circumstances, once a district has a viable strategy, it faces two central capacity-building challenges. The first is delivering excellence when the scale is vast, in terms of students, teachers, and administrative and support staff. The second is speed. The capacity of its people must be built at an accelerating pace over time to keep up with the momentum and expectations created by early wins. As Weast puts it, "If investments in knowledge and skill are not made quickly enough or if the pace of change is too fast, then you will overrun your capacity to deliver and the reforms will fail. It is a balancing act."[2] At MCPS this meant radical reorganization of HR activities and deployment of resources to invest in people to align their knowledge and skills with the differentiation strategy.

HUMAN RESOURCES IN MCPS

Investments in the knowledge and skills needed for workforce excellence will have limited effectiveness if a district cannot recruit and retain talented people with the potential and foundational skills to manage a modern, diverse classroom. MCPS competes for the best and brightest in a crowded market for talent in order to fill more than 11,500 teaching and nearly 200 principal spots. The district pays its teachers a competitive starting salary of around $44,000, but it cannot rely solely on compensation to attract talent, because several other adjacent counties pay in the same range. Teachers also receive fully paid training days and opportunities to work up to twenty additional days, but neighboring school districts in Arlington and Fairfax counties offer similar perks.

The union contracts in MPCS are similar to those in most large school districts—the most recent teachers' contract is 129 pages long and covers everything from student discipline and the physical environment to salaries and transfers. Teachers earn tenure after a two-year probationary period. These are similar to the constraints that many district leaders around the country face. One big difference is the culture of respect cultivated among union leaders and district management, even though they still have plenty of disagreements and tough negotiations. This climate is a clear advantage in the recruiting process.

Over time, the long-term investments in workforce capacity have become a competitive advantage in the hiring market as well. The word is out that MCPS is a place that invests in the capacity of its people, which is similar to a phenomenon that often occurs when some of the top companies in the world compete in the global market for talent.

FOCUSING ON TALENT AT ALL LEVELS

When new superintendents take on the leadership of a district, they often bring with them a group of trusted senior staff members that replace many of the existing people, which is an approach that has both strengths and limitations. In contrast, Weast brought no team members along, preferring to give everyone a chance to prove they had the knowledge, skills, and ability to do their job well. As he puts it, "Everyone starts with an A." Despite his positive outlook, however, he has high standards and expects commitment and results.

The 1999–2000 school year began three weeks after Weast arrived at MCPS. The school system had rushed to implement a new student information system. With potential year 2000 (Y2K) problems on the horizon, MCPS, like many organizations, decided to replace the old student information system rather make the existing system Y2K compliant. Unfortunately, the system had not been adequately tested, and the high usage on the first days of school almost brought it to a halt. Because response times were too long, schools were unable to enroll students, change schedules, or take attendance. The meltdown hit a low point the day President Bill Clinton and other dignitaries visited Brook Grove Elementary School. Weast was not satisfied with the responsiveness of his IT staff or with the explanations he received about the failure of the system. Within a week, the head of IT was terminated for his performance.

A number of individuals in executive staff positions decided to leave MCPS during Weast's first year. Before the end of Weast's first year, the deputy superintendent left the system. Others in high-level positions also left as the superintendent began to build his team around his rigorous expectations. It became crystal clear that implementing wide-ranging initiatives would take considerable time and commitment. Several leadership positions became open as some took superintendent positions in other school systems, others retired, and some left of their own volition. The changes helped to set the stage for reform by creating an opportunity to recruit and select people who had not only the skills necessary for their roles, but a disposition toward rapid change and improvement.

The district's hiring system had long been criticized for being ineffective, leading to significant numbers of open teaching positions every year. This, coupled with new teaching positions created by dramatically smaller class sizes in the Red Zone early grades, meant that MCPS needed a better way to find talented people to fill the vacant and recently created positions. The HR department streamlined its hiring process and implemented open contracts, year-round recruiting, and a "grow your own talent" plan in partnership with local universities. MCPS began to aggressively seek out teacher candidates through formalized programs developed to source a candidate pipeline that more closely mirrored the demographics of the district's students and to recruit and retain teachers in high-need schools. The new processes, procedures, and relationships transformed the human resources function.

CREATING A PROFESSIONAL LEARNING ENVIRONMENT

Creating professional development that supports a strategy for improvement takes money, time, and focused effort. The investment has paid off—children in MCPS are making remarkable gains—but the MCPS leadership team had to deliver on the promises of increased academic achievement in order to continue the flow of funds for training and sustain stakeholder support. That took building the skills of teachers to deliver a rigorous curriculum in ways that allow students of different readiness levels to succeed. To accomplish this, MCPS developed a number of initiatives, including a Professional Growth System (PGS), Peer Assistance and Review (PAR), staff development teachers, and a Professional Learning Communities Institute. Yet before any of these could achieve their potential, Weast had to lay a strong foundation for professional learning in MCPS—first by emphasizing collaboration and then by restructuring departments.

In April 1997, before Weast arrived, the board of education awarded a contract to Research for Better Teaching (RBT), a training and consulting firm dedicated to improving teaching and student achievement, to work with the school system to develop a new teacher evaluation system. Instead of simply replacing the old evaluation system, the board approved the development and deployment of a Professional Growth System. Among other things, the PGS included an evaluation system, clear standards for performance, a common language and framework for teaching, and a Peer Assistance and Review program to provide intensive support for brand-new teachers and underperforming teachers. Representatives from the teachers and administrators unions and central office staff worked with RBT to design the system.

By the time Weast arrived in Montgomery County in August 1999, considerable work had been done. In chapter 3, we discussed the interactions between union leaders and Weast as they worked together to resolve issues related to the design the PGS, which became an overarching framework for teacher development. The collaborative work on the PGS also began to establish norms of how the district management and the three unions might work together on investments in people, and in a way built a new capacity for partnering on important issues.

Along with building the capacity for the groups to work together, Weast decided to restructure how that training would be delivered. When he first arrived, responsibility for professional development was distributed throughout the system. There was a Department of Staff Development, which was responsible for leadership training, continuing education and tuition reimbursement programs, new teacher training, staff development, and university partnerships. But other offices did their own training. The curriculum and instruction office trained teachers on new or revised curriculum; the special education department did almost all of the training of special education teachers and assistants; and the English for Speakers of Other Languages (ESOL) department trained ESOL teachers.

Frustrated with this fragmentation, Weast asked the associate superintendents to develop a reorganization plan that would bring all of the training under the responsibility of an Office of Organizational Development. Eventually the head of the office became an associate superintendent and a member of the superintendent's executive leadership team. After convincing county council members to provide additional funding for professional development, Weast tripled the percentage of the budget that went to training and development from 1 percent to 3 percent, or approximately $50 million. While still less than the standard private sector practice of investing as much as 10 percent of operating budgets in human capital development, the increase was a dramatic improvement over historical spending patterns in MCPS and more aggressive than most large school districts in the United States.

Now, with a direct reporting relationship to the superintendent and considerable financial resources, the new Office of Staff Development (OSD) had tremendous power within MCPS, but it also had an enormous responsibility. The group was expected to ensure that *all* professional development in MCPS was aligned with its strategy for improvement and that resources were used strategically and effectively—no small task.

INVESTING IN THE SKILLFUL TEACHER

With the foundation for a high-quality professional development system in place, Weast's first step was to bring a common training experience to all teachers. In collaboration with Research for Better Teaching, the district provided Skillful Teacher courses for teachers and administrators. Skillful Teacher is a well-established program focused on developing teachers' capacities to recognize and respond to learning differences among students. The program also has a heavy emphasis on the impact of high expectations and quality instruction on student learning. Using the existing Skillful Teacher framework, RBT and MCPS worked together to create an integrated approach that incorporated general and MCPS-specific content regarding standards, instructional strategies, assessment, differentiation, data analysis, use of data systems and technology, and more. Ten

additional trainers were hired to ensure that all teachers and principals could access the courses. Because of the sequenced implementation of the differentiation strategy described in chapter 2, elementary
teachers in the Red Zone schools were the first cohort to go through
Skillful Teacher training. Over time, it was spread to every teacher in
the district.

One of the most important contributions of the initiative was that
it helped create throughout the district—across content and grade
levels—a united view about the characteristics and importance of
high-quality teaching and learning and its link to student outcomes.
In addition to technical practices, the program focused on teachers'
and administrators' beliefs about students and their ability to learn
and grow versus having been "born smart." One teacher describes it
this way: "I think it ('Skillful Teacher') had a huge impact . . . just the
whole theory about 'effort' and us switching to believe that you are
not just smart because you were born smart. It just kind of brought
it to [our consciousness], effort and hard work. You have to put in a
lot of effort, and working hard makes you smarter. I think that the
students were getting that consistently throughout [my] building. We
believe in you. You can do this."[3]

The program also focused on the impact of expectations on students learning. Teacher expectations were defined as inferences that
teachers make about the future academic achievement of a student.
Schoolwide expectations were defined as the beliefs held by the staff
as a whole about the learning ability of the student body. The program also provided specific staff behaviors and instructional practices
that would serve as evidence of high expectations. These ideas began
to permeate the language of teachers and administrators in MCPS.

As Weast describes it, "Skillful Teacher wasn't just about how to
teach. It gave us a common way of thinking and talking about teaching and learning and experiencing it together across the district."[4] The
enormous investment in the Skillful Teacher program was about more
than just improving technical skills—it also was about changing the
districtwide culture.

LAUNCHING A PROFESSIONAL GROWTH SYSTEM

The foundation of professional development in MCPS was the launch in 2000 of the Professional Growth System for teachers. The PGS had broad support given that the unions had been working to create it before Weast arrived, and he had played a productive and unusual role in mediating disagreements between union leaders in his early days on the job. District and union leaders shared the goal of raising student achievement by increasing the skills of classroom teachers (both new and veteran) through the creation of a comprehensive professional development plan. They sought to design a system that included features of both accountability and learning: there would be high expectations and a high degree of support. The PGS would support teacher growth, and the Peer Assistance and Review system would identify underperforming teachers. The major components of the Montgomery County PGS for teachers are:

- A common language and framework for teaching.

- Job-embedded professional development provided by staff development teachers located at each school site.

- Time for teachers to participate in professional development opportunities.

- Teacher-directed personal growth through personal development plans.

- A Peer Assistance and Review program to provide more intensive support for new teachers and underperforming experienced teachers.

- A teacher evaluation system based on standards of effective practice from the National Board for Professional Teaching Standards.

As often as possible, MCPS combined training and coaching in different but related areas to create the more integrated experiences that adult learners need in order to better synthesize and apply new skills and knowledge in their daily work—in this case, in their classrooms with their diverse groups of students. Flexibility was another feature of the system. Teachers would receive much of the training on-site rather than trekking off to remote conference centers for hours at a time. This on-site process was managed by school principals. To provide time for teachers to participate fully while ensuring ongoing instruction for students, the district created a substitute program in which substitute teachers were contracted in advance to step in during staff development periods. This allowed teams of teachers to experience training together, even if the focus was on individual skill building.

As we mentioned in chapter 2, with the passage of the curriculum policy in 2001, the board set the expectation that the goal of teacher professional development was to prepare teachers to teach the written curriculum. Thus, direction came from the top, but teachers were not just told to go and make it happen. A variety of resources were put in place to support this renewed attention to the established curriculum. The district added 142 new positions in the form of a staff development teacher for each school. The staff development teacher worked with the school staff as a whole to develop a professional learning community and helped every teacher develop an individual professional development plan (PDP). Placing support in the schools also increased teachers' sense of control over the resources, time, and materials being invested to help them develop.

In addition to the staff development teachers, teacher team leaders, content coaches, and other positions were established at the site level to help teachers improve instruction. These positions included content experts in math at the elementary level and Algebra 1 specialists. These positions were also part of a different aspect of teacher development, a pathway to leadership positions called the *career lattice*, which is the last component of the PGS and is still under development. The career lattice is specifically designed to attract and retain high-performing teachers in the highest-need schools. The first entry into the lattice is being designated as a lead teacher, as determined by a joint panel of teachers and administrators. This designation will make a teacher eligible for leadership positions such as consulting teacher, content specialist, and literacy coach. Teachers become eligible to enter the lattice only after five years of successful teaching experience and fulfillment of specific professional development requirements.

Alongside the PGS, the Peer Assistance and Review program was begun in 2002. As a part of PAR, consulting teachers provide instructional support to novice teachers and those not performing to standard. The goal was to create a collaborative learning culture among teachers in each school, integrating individual growth plans into school plans. PAR was not developed and implemented overnight; it was phased in over a three-year period. Mark Simon and Ed Shirley, presidents of the teachers and administrators unions, worked with Larry Bowers, the MCPS chief operating officer, to create PAR. Bonnie Cullison and Rebecca Newman succeeded Shirley and Simon and, in partnership with Bowers, crafted a program that would hold teachers to high standards, support those who needed guidance and new skills, and let go of those not able to make the grade. Initially, there was a great deal of resistance to this idea. Teachers were concerned about peer review; it went against their value of egalitarianism and their core beliefs about the purpose of unions and what being a professional meant. Over time, however, teachers have seen positive results and have warmed to the program.

So how does the PAR program work? In a given year, MCPS hires between 850 and 1,200 new teachers, about half of whom have never taught before. All new teachers are observed five or six times during their first year by a consulting teacher and are given advice about areas where they can improve the quality of their teaching. For a novice teacher, feeling alone in the classroom and unsure of his skills, such assistance can be invaluable. At the end of the first year, a PAR panel of teachers and administrators reviews the consulting teacher and principal's recommendations and decides whether or not to retain the novice teacher. After the second year, the novice teacher is reviewed again, this time by only his principal. The teacher is granted tenure if he successfully passes both evaluations.

The situation is different for experienced or tenured teachers, who become part of the PAR process only if their principal determines that their performance is not meeting expectations. Once the PAR process is initiated, a consulting teacher reviews the teacher's skills and assesses the problem. If the consulting teacher determines that the teacher should be part of the PAR program, a yearlong intervention plan is initiated. At the end of the year—during which the teacher has been given tips, support, model lessons, and other assistance—the consulting teacher offers an independent evaluation and recommendation. The joint panel of teachers and administrators then makes a decision about whether or not to retain the teacher.

In the first four years of the PAR system, about 500 underperforming teachers were assigned to the system. Of that group, 177 new and veteran teachers were dismissed, were not renewed, or resigned. By contrast, from 1994 to 1999, before the PAR system was in place, MCPS dismissed only one teacher due to performance issues.

The remaining 323 struggling teachers were able to raise their performance and retain their jobs. Since PAR's inception, consulting teachers have served over 2,200 teachers who were new to the district. The teachers union acknowledges the link between the PGS and its impact on teacher quality, and believes in the ability of PAR to strengthen its members' skills, thereby increasing the effectiveness of the overall improvement strategy. MCEA–MCPS alignment around professional standards for teachers is a powerful force for building districtwide capacity.

Despite the commitment to the process, many principals and other leaders are uncomfortable telling teachers and other staff that they aren't doing well, particularly if they are long-term employees. For the system to be successful, however, peer evaluation and review is necessary. The support of experienced consulting teachers who help their colleagues craft more-powerful instructional approaches and develop new teaching strategies helps MCPS build a workforce that speaks a common language, understand its goals, and is prepared to achieve success.

Soon after implementation of the PGS for teachers was under way, the MCPS leadership team agreed during negotiations with the administrators union—the Montgomery County Association of Administrative and Supervisory Personnel (MCAASP)—that a new growth and evaluation system for administrators was sorely needed. Instead of using an outside organization like RBT, central services staff and union leadership agreed to pull together a committee with representatives of both groups and facilitate the work themselves.

The MCAASP president, Rebecca Newman, agreed to cochair a new committee with COO Bowers, and supported the idea that representatives of all unions could participate along with parent and student representatives and staff from central office departments. Newman had been an administrator and high school principal for more than twenty-five years and was widely respected by her colleagues. Bob Bastress, a sitting high school principal, was selected to facilitate this new process and eventually took on the role full-time. He was extremely skilled in using an interest-based process to get the group to reach consensus on many difficult issues. Together, they created a PGS that began with principals and then extended to assistant principals and central services administrators so that all administrators would have standards for performance and growth. Its major components are:

- Processes for identifying, encouraging, and developing potential leaders from within.

- Differentiated professional development opportunities for novice administrators, administrators new to MCPS, and veteran administrators.

- Time for administrators to participate in professional development opportunities.

- Administrator-designed personal growth through personal development plans.

- Access to mentors.

- An evaluation system based on six leadership standards. The standards, professional development opportunities, and system goals are all aligned. The standards, and their corresponding performance criteria, define the role of the site administrator.

As with some of the other activities in MCPS, many districts have lists of standards or competencies for administrators. What distinguishes them from the others is that there is a system in place to use the list to evaluate the performance of principals, as well as a deliberate, disciplined effort to link the attributes to the elements of the improvement strategy.

In 2006, the district expanded the PGS to include support services personnel. The Supporting Service Professional Growth System (SSPGS) addressed the recruitment, staffing, evaluation, development, retention, and recognition of all supporting services staff, which includes more than 500 job classifications, with positions ranging from bus operators to mechanics to teacher assistants. As in the PGS for teachers and administrators, supporting services staff members are regularly evaluated on a set of core competencies: commitment to students, knowledge of the job, professionalism, interpersonal skills, communication, organization, and problem solving. Extending the PGS to noninstructional staff was an enormous step toward integrating all of the professional energy in the district to strengthen the important work that happens in classrooms. In fact, the training and professional growth plans for supporting service employees have resulted in 235 staff members being promoted to supervisors and classroom teachers. MCPS is growing its own talent and promoting them through the ranks.

Each of the PGS systems includes a PAR component, and representatives from MCAASP sit on the panels of all three. Given that principals manage the implementation of the PGS in schools and all three employee groups work together closely in schools to improve student learning, this integrated approach to professional growth is key to the success of the programs.

PROFESSIONAL LEARNING COMMUNITIES INSTITUTE

MCPS and the three unions also worked together to create the Professional Learning Communities Institute (PLCI) to help elementary schools develop high-performing teams that could work together to improve student performance. PLCI was led by Jamie Virga, a long-time teacher and the former principal of Viers Mill Elementary, a rousing success in the early days of the Red Zone Early Success initiative. His appointment was central to the theory behind the project: school teams had much to learn from other organizations inside and outside the district that could help them accelerate progress for their students. Because the district believed that schools would improve faster if teams of adults worked together to diagnose and respond to the needs of diverse learners, PLCI was a team-based experience.

As a first step, an internal team wrote case studies on three MCPS schools: Broad Acres, Ronald McNair, and Viers Mill Elementary. All three schools had experienced dramatic success with the new strategy, and the case studies discussed effective practices—processes, strategies, beliefs, and tools—that had been put in place to increase and sustain student performance in each of these highly successful schools.

Schools apply to participate, and each year PLCI accepts ten or eleven sites. Teams of twelve to fifteen educators from each school convene to read business and education case studies (including the three on the MCPS elementary schools) to reflect on their own situation, and to create plans for action. One principal commented on the team-based approach: "PLCI gives us the opportunity for the larger team to have time to work together. This includes the administration, teachers, supporting services, and parents. Everyone comes together to form agreements through the process of consensus. Everyone's involved in a decision-making process to improve the quality of student education."[5]

The teams meet for one full day every two months. The goal of the sessions is for the teams to work together to apply what they have learned by designing an action plan for their individual schools. For educators participating in the institute, the sessions have been powerful catalysts for change. Seeing the results from schools within the same district with similar resources and student populations was a powerful experience for school teams. As one executive leadership team member explained it, "I think the greatest symbol was what happened with Broad Acres. When your most impacted school, 99% minority and approximately 90% poverty, becomes one of your highest-performing schools, it's hard for any other school to say that minorities can't do well."[6] In chapter 6, we will look more closely at the Broad Acres story, along with those of other schools.

Between the strategy sessions, participating schools are given ongoing, specific support for their action plans via site visits or phone consultations with the PLCI staff. All PLCI schools are also eligible to apply for a grant of up to $10,000 that can be used to support collaborative teaching, academic interventions, and school-community partnerships.

EXECUTIVE TEAM DEVELOPMENT

As the professional development systems for teachers, administrators, and support staff were being planned and implemented, Weast turned his attention toward increasing the capacity of his executive team. As a veteran superintendent, he knew that there were few opportunities for top-level district administrators to share with and learn from each other. The job of an associate superintendent, chief operating officer, or human resource director can be a lonely one.

In 2003, Weast learned of a newly developed program for urban district teams offered jointly by Harvard Business School and Harvard Graduate School of Education. Called the Public Education Leadership Project (PELP), the project was initially a three-year commitment by Harvard and nine large districts to an annual cycle of field research on the challenges of district leadership teams, content development that was relevant to those challenges, and a one-week summer executive education program that included discussions of business cases and newly developed education cases. The weeklong experience also included team strategy sessions facilitated by Harvard professors to help districts build leadership capacity and formulate a coherent districtwide strategy.

Weast selected a team of seven leaders, including a union president and a board member, to attend the program with him. Through the experience, participants developed their own leadership and analytical skills, but as a team, they also began to understand the importance of aligning systems, structures, culture, resources, and stakeholders around an improvement strategy that focuses on high-quality teaching and learning. Since the initial three-year commitment ended, Weast has continued to send new teams to PELP each summer, gradually moving across and down the hierarchy of MCPS to broaden access to the ideas and to build a common language. In chapter 6 we will discuss the specific impact the experience had on MCPS's approach to breaking the link between race and academic outcomes.

As Weast created new positions or experienced openings on his executive team, he filled them with principals who had achieved success with the differentiation strategy. As we mentioned earlier, Jamie Virga from Viers Mill launched the PLCl and later became head of the Office of Organizational Development. Jody Leleck, the principal of the highly successful Broad Acres Elementary, eventually became the district's chief academic officer, and Stephen Bedford, principal of Gaithersburg High School, became a community superintendent and went on to head the Office of School Performance. This strengthened the central office capacity to support the work of school teams that were implementing the district strategy on the front lines by promoting leaders who were respected by their peers for having done it themselves. It also sent a signal that success at MCPS meant breaking the link between race and achievement, and that success would be rewarded.

LOOKING FOR INNOVATIVE SOLUTIONS

As MCPS looks to the future, it must find more effective and efficient ways to dramatically improve staff capacity in some areas. For instance, with a goal of 80 percent of all students completing algebra by the end of eighth grade, nearly every middle school math teacher must be skilled at delivering high-level content. This creates an enormous human capital challenge for the system. In the old sorting model, only some students were deemed smart enough for algebra in middle school, so schools only needed a few elite math teachers. In the new MCPS, increasing the skills of existing teachers has to go along with recruiting new teachers prepared to teach higher-level math to middle schoolers. Given that even in the old tiered system great math teachers are in short supply all over the country, this is a significant challenge for MCPS.

The district is in talks with Lockheed Martin's Simulation, Training and Support (STS) group to create a prototype of a potentially breakthrough approach to teacher training. Lockheed has a significant business presence in Montgomery County and has long been an active supporter of the MCPS strategy. Brian Edwards, the superintendent's chief of staff, is managing discussions about the development of a new approach to algebra professional development that builds on STS's sophisticated simulation and gaming technology, used by the military and commercial sectors to prepare people for complex and often high-risk professional tasks. The project is in the very early stages, but the general idea is that teachers could practice proven instructional techniques for core algebra skills in a virtual classroom environment that would include students with a variety of learning needs. In addition to creating a safe environment for teachers to learn and try out new skills, it has the potential to provide training to more teachers at a faster pace, using fewer resources. The talks are ongoing, and MCPS is committed to looking for new ways to invest in the capacity of its people to create success for students within the district strategy of differentiated delivery of rigorous content.

CONCLUSION

MCPS created professional standards that made high expectations concrete for all district employees, and followed through on a reciprocal commitment to invest in the capacity building necessary to help people meet those standards. The district took a broad view of professional development, realizing that adults usually learn to do things better by doing them, not by listening to a lecture or reading about them. By creating multiple roles that support teachers and administrators in active learning, they have dramatically improved the district's capacity to provide excellence and equity to all students.

MCPS has a clear strategy in place, and the professional development systems and structures, such as the PGS, PAR, and PLCI, are coherent with that strategy. The challenge is to create an environment in which excellence and equity increase at an ever-accelerating pace. While this can be accomplished over time by refining targets and steadily asking for more from students, teachers, and leaders, the infrastructure must be in place to help everyone succeed. One of Weast's frequent observations is that his biggest challenge is to manage the tension between the pace necessary to meet ambitious targets and the capacity of the system to implement the strategy. In chapter 5 we will explore more of the systems and structures that MCPS implemented to support its investments in people and its commitment to breaking the link between race, class, and academic outcomes.

CHAPTER FIVE

Designing New Systems and Structures for Change

The district had to build new ways of working ... that would accelerate the ability of teachers and administrators to diagnose performance problems, differentiate their approaches to solving them, and constantly reflect and adapt as they learned more about how to address the learning needs of their students.

MCPS designed a strategy to break the link between race, ethnicity, and academic outcomes by setting common, aggressive standards and by differentiating resources and instruction so that all students could reach them. The district built relationships and invested heavily in developing the knowledge and skill of individuals and teams to expand the organization's capacity to implement the strategy. For this to pay off over the long term, Weast knew that the district needed to institutionalize the new approach to achieving results. One of Weast's abilities is to understand that in a complex system such as a school district, everything connects to everything else. Instead of being unnerved by it, he used the insight to make the organization more powerful and sustainable. Indeed, that is the difference between systemic and piecemeal change. The irony, of course, is that all lasting change is systemic—a change in any part of the system ripples through the system as a whole, affecting each part differently, for better or worse.

In order to create systemic change, school and central office teams began the hard work of tearing down institutional barriers to rigorous content that reinforced long-standing inequities among students, as discussed in chapters 1 and 2. In their place, the district had to build new ways of working—systems and structures—that would accelerate the ability of teachers and administrators to diagnose performance problems, differentiate their approaches to solving them, and constantly reflect and adapt as they learned more about how to address the learning needs of their students.

Once again, Our Call to Action played a vital role in framing the task for MCPS. The 1999 strategic blueprint suggested improvements in systems and structures to raise the bar and close the gap:

- There is a systemwide need for user-friendly (and user-useful) information and data analysis to shape thinking, learning, and problem solving.

- It is imperative to provide instructional software, equipment, and corresponding staff development. These tools are needed to foster students' critical thinking, reading, and writing skills; enable multiple paths for learning and communicating; and provide differentiated instruction.

- Resources have to be reorganized to provide maximum support for teaching and learning.

ANALYSIS, PLANNING, ACTION, AND REFLECTION

The district started on its plan to set up districtwide processes for planning, action, and reflection and the infrastructure to support those changes. During his first year, the school board endorsed Weast's plan to reorganize the MCPS's central administration. The reorganization was designed to support student achievement by focusing system assets and resources directly on schools. According to the new plan, clusters of schools would be supported by a matrix of teams, each reporting to one of six community superintendents. This new system was in marked contrast to the old structure in which principals had run their schools for several years with very little oversight or support and without a clear districtwide strategy. The new community superintendents were charged with ensuring that the new strategy was implemented by the schools in their cluster and that principals had what they needed to be successful—ultimately, they were accountable for their cluster's performance. Principals in a given cluster were accountable to their community superintendent, who could differentiate his or her management approach based on the needs of the various school leaders. Weast also created three deputy superintendent–level positions, which eventually dropped to two by year's end, to oversee academics, organizational development, and operations.

With the structural changes in place, Weast initiated a district self-assessment in the fall of 2000 using the Malcolm Baldrige Education Criteria for Performance Excellence. The Baldrige quality system included a continuous improvement process and quality indicators for various industries, including manufacturing, service, small business, education, health care, and nonprofit, and was named for former secretary of commerce and proponent of quality improvement Malcolm Baldrige. Each year since 1987, organizations in each of these industries have been eligible to receive the Baldrige Award for Quality, which has spurred a broader quality improvement movement around its criteria. In education, customized quality indicators for leadership, strategic planning, customer focus, workforce focus, process management, results, and measurement, analysis, and knowledge management are designed to guide districts toward higher performance. Weast used these world-class standards to identify the district's strengths and weaknesses, and to unearth opportunities for improvement. The process centered the district staff's attention on understanding the model and set the stage for its application across the district.

In order to make the most of the findings from the assessment, MCPS created a Baldrige Leadership Team, consisting of representatives from multiple stakeholders, which served as a driving force behind implementing the findings that emerged from the initial self-assessment. The team met monthly to assess progress and determine how implementation could be more effective. One outcome of these meetings was a decision to adopt the Baldrige analysis framework for every level of the district. All central office departments were required to adopt a plan/do/study/act improvement cycle for developing annual plans in an effort to systematize data-driven decision making at the headquarters level. The board of education adopted the framework to help guide its own work. The existing annual school planning process was adapted to the Baldrige model so that everyone had a common language and approach for identifying performance challenges and responding to them. Each school created a School Improvement Team that included teachers, parents, and support staff, and students at the high school level. The team took collective responsibility for implementing its school's plan. In order to develop the skills of school teams to use the model, the district created three "Baldrige Academy" schools: Waters Landing and Sherwood Elementary schools and Tilden Middle School. At each of these schools, teachers who had been trained in the use of Baldrige quality tools in the classroom provided workshops for teachers at other schools on a scheduled basis.

The plan/do/study/act language was incorporated into the supervisory interactions between principals and teachers, as well as between community superintendents and principals. In the course of a few years, MCPS developed a common system for creating districtwide implementation plans and school-level plans that were consistent with the overall district goals. The consistent focus from the system level to the individual school level was raising performance for all students while accelerating the rate of improvement for the students who were farthest behind. Every school had the flexibility to create its own plans for differentiating its approach to meet its students' needs, but had to use the districtwide standards and planning process.

In the early 1990s, MCPS had deployed a student data monitoring tool called SIMS, which principals had been enthusiastic about, and the heightened focus on data use through the Baldrige model helped accelerate the demand for frequent, reliable data that would allow for better differentiation based on specific student learning needs. Weast and the board committed to building the technology infrastructure that could collect, store, and analyze all of the data that staff around the district needed to be successful.

STRATEGIC INVESTMENTS IN TECHNOLOGY

Weast was a believer in the promise of technology to support the district's drive for excellence and equity, but he knew MCPS didn't have the expertise that it needed to create the technical infrastructure that would support teachers' and administrators' need for the data necessary to make decisions about differentiated resources and instruction. So Weast made what was seen as a bold move at the time—he hired a chief information officer (CIO), John Q. Porter. While CIOs were ubiquitous in the private sector by 2000, they were rare in public education. With a background in business technology, Porter had a difficult job ahead of him. To be successful, he had to blend the technical side of his position with knowledge about good curriculum and instruction. Among other things, Porter had to ensure that any technology implemented was both useful and user friendly. One of his first big decisions was to decide whether MCPS would buy, build, or blend its technology infrastructure. At the time, school information technology was in its infancy; indeed, much of it was repurposed business (and sometimes military) software, not well suited to school needs or activities. Because of this, the district decided to use a combination of building from scratch and blending off-the-shelf systems with MCPS's own technology.

In 2002, MCPS developed and began implementing an Integrated Quality Management System (IQMS), a comprehensive knowledge management system that would enable the combination of instructional data with professional development, financial, human resource, and other key data to inform decisions. The IQMS eventually included the Instructional Management System (IMS), a districtwide data warehouse, and a student information system to manage all student administrative data, including enrollment, attendance, special education information, grades, scheduling, and course management.

The IMS was designed to be a tactical tool for administrators and teachers. It is a set of Web-based tools designed to manage and deliver curricula, monitor student performance on formative and summative assessments and gifted and talented screenings, and provide the data required to support No Child Left Behind. For example, it allows teachers to access curriculum guides, lesson plans, and individual student performance from any networked computer. As such, administrators and teachers are able to modify instruction and develop learning plans tailored to the needs of specific children.

The data warehouse, which was rolled out in 2003, was to be used as a strategic tool. It was designed to permit the evaluation of which key initiatives and strategies helped achieve district goals. With the launch of the data warehouse, school and district administrators gained the capacity to investigate student learning outcomes over time in comparison to other schools and other groups of students. Educators use this data to create their school improvement plans through the Baldrige process, which includes identifying focus areas for differentiated instruction and monitoring the academic achievement trends of individual and groups of students. The system continually updates summary and student-level performance information on a school-by-school basis, and includes a graphically depicted decision model that displays data aggregated at the school, cluster, and county level.

As Porter commented in 2005, "We wanted to create a knowledge management system that not only captures all the information we need, but also turns this information into knowledge to inform and drive staff decisions . . . By providing easy access to individual performance data, we hope to help teachers save time and support them in focusing and tailoring their instruction to match a child's needs."[1]

In addition to these system-level tools, MCPS invested in tools that teachers could use every day to diagnose and respond to their students' real-time performance data. In the interest of space, we will describe only a few of the tools the district developed, beginning with a partnership focused on assessing early-elementary reading achievement with the private handheld technology company Wireless Generation.

As early as 2002, the district had been using its own predictive reading assessment for K–2, called the MCPS Assessment Program Primary Reading (APPR), in 129 of its elementary schools. However, Weast and Porter wanted to develop a custom application that would put APPR on handheld devices for teachers so MCPS could electronically track students' reading progress leading up to grade 3. Porter explained, "Automating our internal assessment on a handheld device meant that teachers didn't have to manually juggle a pencil, paper, and a stopwatch while listening to readers. It would free up time for teachers to do higher-level tasks with students. It also meant that we could electronically capture all the assessment data on every child in every classroom and analyze it. This would not only help teachers differentiate their instruction for their students but allow the district to differentiate professional development for teachers."[2]

In order to accomplish this, MCPS constructed a joint venture with Wireless Generation that led to the creation of a product called mCLASS:Reading 3D, a software application on a personal digital assistant (PDA) device that enables teachers to do comprehensive literacy assessments and capture the data instantaneously in a student's electronic file. The technology permits teachers to assess a child's reading skills in depth and takes into account both whole-language and phonetic approaches to reading. Teachers are able to ascertain a fuller picture of a student's needs because Reading 3D gauges phonemic awareness, letter recognition, fluency, and writing, among other things.

Teachers began to use the product to assess students' skills in grades K–2 in the nineteen Red Zone elementary schools that continued to serve as innovation labs for piloting new initiatives. If the pilot were successful, MCPS would roll out the tool to all elementary schools over two years. Although the pilot teachers reported that technical aspects of the implementation were smooth, there were some areas that caused frustration. For example, the APPR had allowed teachers to decide when to stop the assessment, but the Reading 3D software automatically determined a stopping point. Ann Bedford, director of curriculum projects, managed the pilot for MCPS. She had spent twelve years as a classroom teacher and another decade as an instructional specialist before taking her current role, so she had a nu-anced understanding of the teaching culture in the district. In reflect-ing on the frustration of some teachers in the pilot, she explained:

> I had a series of difficult conversations with a second-grade teacher who was having trouble accepting the judgments of the software. He kept arguing with me that he knew a particular kid couldn't perform at the level the technology required. He said, "Why should I even waste my time and waste his time? I know he can't do it." Finally after several conversations, I looked at him and said very firmly, "No matter what you believe about this student, at some point in time when you admin-ister the test he *is* going to be able to do it, and you're not going to know that until you try it." And he didn't have any response to that.[3]

In March Weast was so pleased with the pilot that he accelerated the rollout. He decided that instead of phasing the product in over the next two years, all elementary schools would have it by the time school opened in September, only a few months away. Throughout the spring and summer, teachers attended training sessions while the MCPS technology team installed the necessary hardware in classrooms.

The accelerated process created snags—the administration had wanted to save teachers time and create a more efficient data analysis process, but teachers said the new assessment process was too slow. In the pilot, this had not been a problem; teachers were adept at using the technology from an earlier pilot. But in September teachers were having trouble using the system. The technology team went into the classrooms and observed that teachers were spending twenty to thirty minutes developing a baseline for *each* child. Weast agreed with Bon-nie Cullison of the teachers union that the district would provide a high-quality substitute teacher to cover the classroom while the teach-ers did the baseline assessments.

In retrospect, Bedford reflected, "With more time maybe we could have communicated more fully and clearly with stakeholders—teach-ers and principals. Much of the push back in the rapid rollout came—I believe—because we didn't take the time to explain well enough how it was linked to instructional improvement. Our teachers and administrators are great and they are focused on their students' learning, but many are naturally intimidated by technology. Maybe if we had moved more slowly we could have built the buy-in at the school level for why this product was so important for students."[4]

Weast acknowledged the misstep, saying, "This is a clear example of requiring a pace of change that overran the capacity of our teachers because we were so aggressive in our rollout efforts. By taking a time-out, listening to our teachers and their union leadership, we were able to recover from the mistake and restart the implementation process in a way that led to greater success."[5] As the staff became more comfortable with the product and MCPS worked through the technical and cultural issues, they began to embrace the idea that they could improve the reading skills of their students by using Reading 3D. Depending on particular student needs, teachers use the device to monitor kids quarterly or as often as every ten days. Syncing stations in every classroom mean that student diagnostic data is available immediately on the Web. As a result, principals, teachers, and reading coaches can quickly determine which children are at risk. Interventions, support, enhancements, and additional resources can be given to students based on this real-time data.

At the Bel Pre Elementary School, which serves mostly African American and Hispanic students, a reading specialist noted, "Having all the information for all students in each teacher's class in one place lets me see where I need to give support. If I see students stuck at the same text level for three or four weeks, I am able to offer teachers new strategies for working with these kids."[6]

MCPS has produced rapid gains in literacy for all students, and even faster gains for African American, Hispanic, and low-income children. While this is clearly attributable to the hard work and increasing skills of the teachers in classrooms, the mCLASS:Reading 3D tool has been an important technology investment that has served as an accelerant to teachers' efforts to more precisely diagnose their students' needs and respond to them effectively by differentiating their instructional approaches in real time.

GETTING BETTER AT FORECASTING

Because all of the data generated by the literacy tool is stored in the data warehouse, the executive team is able to analyze systemwide trends to better support schools and to set more informed goals. In the introduction to this book, we mentioned that over 90 percent of kindergartners met the district reading benchmark in 2008, and that the benchmark would be more aggressive for 2009. The target for kindergarten reading in 2008 was "text level four," which had been painstakingly negotiated with MCEA and MCAASP. But an analysis by the MCPS research unit of correlations among different indicators stored in the data warehouse showed that students needed to hit level six—not level four—in kindergarten if they were to stay on course on the Pathway to Success in second grade and third grade. Schools were already successfully getting 65 percent of all their students to the more aggressive goal, including 80 percent of white students. The challenge was to find differentiated approaches support African American and Hispanic students in reaching the new goal.

In the 2004–2005 school year, MCPS began administering a computer adaptive achievement test called Measures of Academic Progress Reading (MAP-R) to students in grades 3 to 5. Computer adaptive testing calibrates the degree of difficulty of questions: if the first question is answered accurately, the second is slightly more difficult; subsequent questions are easier or more difficult depending on the answer to the preceding question. With the goal of refining and creating strategies to close the achievement gap, the district decided to look at whether or not the students' MAP-R scores would help principals and teachers identify students at risk of not performing well on state assessments. Indeed, the district found that MAP-R could predict (with 85–90 percent accuracy) the likelihood of a student scoring at proficient or above, or scoring below proficiency standards. Another example is the grade 6, 7, and 8 predictions for the Math MSA (Maryland School Assessment) Model, completed in September 2007. This model provides a prediction of grade 6, 7, and 8 performances for math MSA from data known at the beginning of the year. The prediction model helps teachers identify students who need help early on in order to do well at the end-of-year assessment.

INSTITUTIONALIZING A MATHEMATICS PATHWAY

As school and district leaders became better at forecasting student success, an effort grew out of a middle school reform initiative to develop a clearer districtwide picture of how students should progress through math courses along the pre-K to 12 continuum in order to graduate ready for college and high-wage work. By backward mapping the steps that successful students had already taken to reach advanced high school math courses, the MCPS team thought it could dramatically increase the number of students who would replicate that trajectory. As Weast described it, "We wanted to watch where people had walked across the grass and put the sidewalk there."[7] The overall MCPS Pathway to Success already included algebra before grade 9, and schools were engaged in a number of approaches to meet the district's goal of 80 percent of students hitting that target by 2014. Creating a clear picture of the various paths that led from elementary through middle school on the way to algebra by grade 9 would be helpful to school teams, students, and parents.

After extensive input from principals, teachers, union leaders, students, and parents, the Office of Curriculum and Instruction created a draft built on an earlier graphic of the math trajectory. The new Mathematics Pathway (see figure 5.1) was designed to help parents and families better understand how performance in early-grade math courses influenced the trajectory of students over the long term. It also served as a communication tool inside MCPS, giving school staff in elementary, middle, and high schools the same information about how the K–12 math "value chain" fit together.

The Mathematics Pathway created a system by which every family in the district could understand and advocate for access to rigorous content, even if they weren't fluent in the internal workings of their school. Chief academic officer Jody Leleck described its importance, saying, "We wanted to make sure that parents, staff,

FIG. 5.1 Pathways to Success in Mathematics

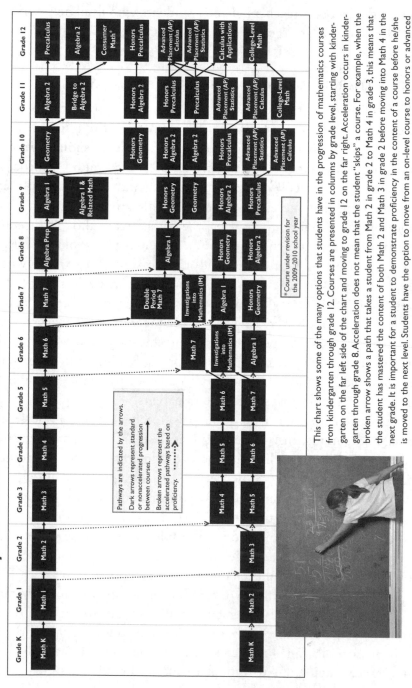

Grade K	Grade 1	Grade 2	Grade 3	Grade 4	Grade 5	Grade 6	Grade 7	Grade 8	Grade 9	Grade 10	Grade 11	Grade 12
Math K	Math 1	Math 2	Math 3	Math 4	Math 5	Math 6	Math 7	Algebra Prep	Algebra 1	Geometry	Algebra 2	Precalculus
									Algebra 1 & Related Math		Bridge to Algebra 2	Algebra 2
												Consumer Math*
							Double Period Math 7			Honors Geometry	Honors Precalculus	Honors Precalculus
						Math 7	Investigations into Mathematics (IM)	Algebra 1	Honors Geometry	Honors Algebra 2	Honors Precalculus	Advanced Placement (AP) Calculus
				Math 5	Math 6	Investigations into Mathematics (IM)	Algebra 1	Honors Geometry	Geometry	Algebra 2	Precalculus	Advanced Placement (AP) Statistics
Math K	Math 2	Math 3	Math 4	Math 6	Math 7	Algebra 1	Honors Geometry	Honors Algebra 2	Honors Precalculus	Honors Precalculus	Advanced Placement (AP) Statistics	Calculus with Applications
										Advanced Placement (AP) Statistics	Advanced Placement (AP) Calculus	College-Level Math
										Advanced Placement (AP) Calculus	College-Level Math	

Pathways are indicated by the arrows.
Dark arrows represent standard or nonaccelerated progression between courses. ⟶
Broken arrows represent the accelerated pathways based on proficiency. ┅┅┅➤

*Course under revision for the 2009–2010 school year

This chart shows some of the many options that students have in the progression of mathematics courses from kindergarten through grade 12. Courses are presented in columns by grade level, starting with kindergarten on the far left side of the chart and moving to grade 12 on the far right. Acceleration occurs in kindergarten through grade 8. Acceleration does not mean that the student "skips" a course. For example, when the broken arrow shows a path that takes a student from Math 2 in grade 2 to Math 4 in grade 3, this means that the student has mastered the content of both Math 2 and Math 3 in grade 2 before moving into Math 4 in the next grade. It is important for a student to demonstrate proficiency in the content of a course before he/she is moved to the next level. Students have the option to move from an on-level course to honors or advanced placement courses at any time throughout high school.

students—everyone really—knew precisely the clearest way to success in math. What we wanted to demonstrate is that no matter where you are on the path, you can get to the high level courses that are going to make sure you are ready for college."[8]

The Mathematics Pathway also allowed for better analysis by school teams as well as the executive leadership team about how minority and low-income students were progressing through coursework necessary for rigorous high school courses.

M-STAT—FOCUSING ON A FEW THINGS THAT MATTER MOST

With several effective new systems in place, the executive team felt it needed a way to pull together all of the information regarding a few indicators that were key to the differentiation strategy so the team could monitor its effectiveness and identify leverage points to accelerate results. In 2004, the leadership group that attended that year's meeting of districts in the Public Education Leadership Project (PELP) at Harvard was impressed by a case that highlighted the New York City Police Department's Computerized Crime Comparison Statistics system (CompStat). Designed by then-commissioner William Bratton and deputy commissioner Jack Maple, CompStat was an effort to use up-to-the-minute data to reduce crime and improve overall precinct performance. Twice a week, precinct commanders met for the CompStat meetings, during which Maple and chief of department Louis Anemone showed individual precinct data to all attendees. Each precinct participated in the process once every five weeks. For crimes in each precinct, the commander was expected to develop a rigorous diagnosis of why the incidents occurred and to present a plan for preventing them. Maple and Anemone would ask pointed questions about the diagnosis and the plan, and if they were not satisfied with the commander's response, he had to return the following week with a more accurate diagnosis and plan. Bratton, Maple, and Anemone emphasized that though the process increased accountability, it was not intended to be punitive; because multiple precincts attended together, it served as a forum for commanders to develop and receive feedback on crime-reducing strategies and to learn from work in other precincts. The MCPS team decided to adapt the system for its own purposes, focusing on a more positive team approach to data-driven decision making. Using the Baldrige problem-solving process plan/do/ study/act and MCPS's own technology and data systems, Weast and his team created a collaborative data-focused process called M-STAT.

By organizing and analyzing data through this process and meeting for in-depth problem-solving discussions, leaders around the district are able to attack key leverage points for continuous improvement. One benefit of M-STAT is that community superintendents can collectively analyze data across schools and work together to find solutions to significant districtwide problems. In fact, rather than launching M-STAT as something the district office would "do to schools," deputy superintendent Frieda Lacey and chief school performance officer Steve Bedford decided to pilot the system by asking community superintendents to engage in guided conversations using data in each of their clusters. All six community superintendents gathered for a rigorous discussion led by Lacey. The first issue they addressed together was PSAT participation and advanced course enrollment of minority students. The data revealed what was widely acknowledged already: even though there was a clear objective to dramatically increase minority participation, it remained low, and there was no strategy in place to change the situation. The team knew that participation in the PSAT meant that a student had the potential to participate in rigorous, high-level courses. PSAT was key to the high school strategy. MCPS had replaced teacher recommendations as the ticket of entry to AP with other indicators, including PSAT scores. This decision increased the importance of PSAT performance. Lacey explained, "Our first efforts were not focused. There was a smorgasbord of strategies being put in place that addressed the total school population even though we had distributed the participation numbers by race and ethnicity. So during that first M-STAT meeting I asked, 'What are you doing specifically for African-American and Hispanic students at schools where the students are mostly white?' The community superintendents were unable to provide me with specific answers, and I told them to bring the information back at the next meeting."[9]

After identifying the problem using the M-STAT process, community superintendents worked with principals and one another to increase the participation of Hispanic and African American students in advanced courses and in the PSAT. In order to boost participation, principals and teachers met with parents and supplied information on the importance of taking the PSAT. Some also made taking the PSAT a better experience by providing food and drinks to students before and after the exam. Community superintendents adopted the M-STAT model with groups of their principals to discuss the PSAT issue. They struggled to make sure the process was safe and not punitive. As one principal noted, "M-STAT also provided the forum for frank discussions and the opportunity for principals to hear about equitable practices that promote high expectations. The positive reinforcement and recognition that schools received from the executives and their peers through the process was unparalleled and was an additional catalyst for both school-wide, then district-wide change. It was to catch us doing something great, not a 'gotcha.'"[10]

Thirteen out of the twenty-four high schools showed an increase in the number of minority kids who were participating in the examination and in more rigorous upper-level classes. But there was still resistance from some schools to place qualified minorities in honors and AP classes.

To overcome the challenge, Lacey created a team led by community superintendent Frank Stetson, formerly a successful high school principal, to develop the Honors/AP Potential Identification Tool (HAPIT). Deputy superintendent Frieda Lacey described its development: "Again, we received pushback and lots of excuses like 'the student didn't make a high enough grade in this course, or they didn't want to move to a higher class,' and so on. So we said to the community superintendents, 'Have we provided them with the research showing that these students have the aptitude for more rigorous classes? And what have we done to let them know we're serious about this?' We then pulled together a work group of staff, principals, and guidance counselors to address the issue, and they came up with the tool HAPIT."[11]

HAPIT allows principals to quickly analyze the potential of students to do AP/honors work, giving principals the ability to compile a list of students who meet specific criteria. In its first version, HAPIT was simply an Excel spreadsheet. The user could find qualified students by using certain markers: ethnicity, PSAT scores, grades, past course enrollments, and performance on specific standardized tests. By March 2006, all secondary principals, guidance counselors, and resource teachers had received HAPIT training.

Even with the tool, some schools were resistant to allowing students to enroll in rigorous classes based on PSAT performance. In order to better understand the complexities of the issue, Lacey decided to visit with the students for whom this was the case: "First I met with a student who had a 4.0 GPA and PSAT scores higher than 44. She said, 'I advocated for myself to be in an AP/honors course, but they told me that classes were full and that I should come back next year.'" After Lacey met with several more students at the same school, word traveled around the district that Lacey was checking in with students who weren't in honors and AP courses despite their high PSAT scores. As Lacey said, "Word had spread fast that we were developing the tool and visiting with students. By early spring, when I made plans to meet with more students, we only found four students who still met the initial criteria."[12] As a consequence, since the initial identification of minority students who had the potential to take part in upper-level coursework, a majority have enrolled in at least one AP or honors course.

The community superintendents continued to work with their principals on using HAPIT, and PSAT participation is increasing—and with a correlated increase in the enrollment numbers for honors and AP courses. By 2008, 88.1 percent of African American and 84.4 percent of Hispanic students took the PSAT, an increase of over 10 percent for both since the 2002–2003 school year. And today, over 60 percent of African American and Hispanic students are enrolled in at least one AP or honors class. MCPS has also taken up a series of other issues in the M-STAT process related to closing the achievement gap. Donna Hollingshead worked closely with Lacey on M-STAT and said of the process, "There was powerful evidence that gap closing strategies not only existed, but worked in the red zone schools. The data showed some red zone schools outperforming the green zone schools (beating the odds). These practices were documented and distributed to all schools. This information provided individual principals the proof they needed to take back to their schools and move their sometimes intractable staffs to reorganize and expand their repertoires to increase student achievement—focusing on narrowing the achievement gap while still hitting or closely approaching district targets."[13]

The M-STAT process has helped create heightened accountability for closing the achievement gap in MCPS, but it has also created a way for evidence about practices that worked in support of the differentiation strategy to spread across the district—not just to Red Zone schools, but into the Green Zone as well. But there is still much to be done. In chapter 6 we will discuss the complex relationship between organizational systems and staff beliefs and behaviors. This is the next frontier of work for MCPS.

CHAPTER SIX

Creating an Equity-Focused Culture

You can't change a school system until there are . . . people in place
that have the same belief system and the right repertoire of skills.
The hard part is, how do you move people to the core beliefs that
[they need]?

Between 1999 and 2005, MCPS made significant progress for students in every subgroup. Chapters 1–5 provide stories about how a
strategy of combining common, rigorous standards with differentiated resources and instruction has the power to change the prospects
of minority and low-income students while continuing to promote excellence throughout the system.[1]

But though the achievement gap on state tests had narrowed by
double digits, absolute performance among minority and low-income
students was still too low. MCPS's rallying cry midway through the
reform journey, "Access + Equity + Rigor = Success," had been embla-
zoned on wall posters and other communications pieces in an effort to
simplify the complexities of the work. Access meant removing barriers and opening doors; equity meant improving training and differentiating instruction; and rigor meant delivering a quality curriculum
aligned with AP and IB course standards. Success means a 100 percent
graduation rate, with 80 percent college and work ready by 2014.

But for all of the communication about expectations and talk about diversity, concrete objectives from 1999's *Our Call to Action*, such as PSAT participation, still needed major attention as late as 2005. Many teachers and principals around the system were working hard to deliver excellence and equity in their schools, but it was unclear whether the culture of high expectations had really taken hold.

In fact, some staff members believed that low expectations of minority students were still pervasive among administrators and teachers of all races. A white staff development teacher shared her perceptions of the state of affairs: "Everyone knows that the politically correct thing to say in Montgomery County is 'every child can learn.' The difference is between those who know the party line and those who believe it. I would say that about one-third believe it in action, one-third isn't sure, and another third don't believe it."

In addition, tension between the MCPS executive leadership team and minority school board members had increased. Newly elected minority board members Nancy Navarro and Valerie Ervin questioned the pace of the implementation of the strategy and the effectiveness of specific initiatives to help African Americans and Hispanics achieve academically. Navarro was a native of Venezuela and had founded Centro Familia, an organization focused on education opportunity and economic development in immigrant communities, prior to her election to the board. Ervin was the dean of students at the National Labor College and would go on to become the first African American woman elected to the county council. Together, they began to increase the attention the school board gave to equity issues.

Many stakeholders considered the performance under Weast's tenure to be tremendous progress, but others agreed with Navarro and Ervin that not enough had changed for minority students since his arrival. The gap between white students and African American and Hispanic students had decreased by over 10 points in nearly every grade between 2004 and 2005, but sizable gaps still remained. The percentage of white students reading at or above proficiency in grade 4 was still more than 10 points higher than that of African American and Hispanic students.

Weast actually shared their desire to accelerate progress, and tried to harness the tension to reinvigorate his team, the school board, union leaders, and staff around the system to do the hard work of analyzing the progress they had made over six years and identifying the remaining barriers to creating a system in which every child would graduate as college and work ready. He reached out to Navarro and Ervin to show them the depth of the work that been done on the race issue thus far and the work that was in progress. Both became ardent supporters of the efforts and understood that it was something that few districts had the courage to pursue.

TALKING ABOUT BELIEFS, WORKING ON BEHAVIORS

MCPS had created a Diversity Training and Development (DTD) initiative within the Office of Organizational Development (OOD), which was responsible for districtwide professional development activities such as Skillful Teacher and the Professional Learning Communities Institute (PLCI). By positioning DTD in OOD, Darlene Merry, associate superintendent for organizational development, thought the group could build the capacity of all OOD staff members to incorporate diversity issues into their work, given that they were responsible for training all of the staff development teachers. The staff development teachers, in turn, delivered the vast majority of professional development to the teachers in their buildings. The approach was built on the premise that four DTD staff members could be leveraged through the rest of the OOD staff and the staff development teachers to virtually every teacher. Donna Graves, who had begun teaching in MCPS in 1969 and now led the DTD, believed in embedding cultural competency into every training session offered to administrators, teachers, supporting services, and other district staff. DTD also offered stand-alone training. The sessions covered such topics as practical strategies to make content accessible to English Language Learners, communicating high expectations to all students, and literacy instruction for African American adolescents. DTD also developed online modules based on *Courageous Conversations*, a well-regarded book by diversity consultant Glenn Singleton.

In addition to its work with staff development teachers, DTD had the capacity to work directly with a limited number of school teams if their principals committed to a diversity training series for one year. Even with the principals' commitment, teacher participation in diversity training was voluntary. While some felt that the training should be mandatory for teachers, others warned that a top-down strategy could backfire. Merry noted that "in the past when the district required school staff to take [certain] training, teachers resisted, and the effectiveness of the training was compromised. Training has always been most effective when teachers and whole schools elected to participate on their own. Building commitment, not compliance, has become a hallmark of our work."

Despite the high "relevance" and "satisfaction with training" ratings given by participants of the group's diversity training sessions, DTD employees worried that they were "preaching to the choir." They believed in the effectiveness of the sessions' content, but they were concerned that teachers and principals who needed diversity training the most did not seek it out. One African American administrator remarked in 2005, "I don't think MCPS has truly committed to take some very serious steps to ensure that students of color, students of poverty, and students with disabilities get the support they need to be successful in schools. It's not consistent in the work that we do. There are some community superintendents who have taken diversity training seriously and have really done a good job in reaching their principals, but it doesn't go throughout. And only a few schools have made a commitment to work on diversity training."

Conversations with teachers and administrators around that time revealed a wide range of views and beliefs about students, some of them inconsistent with the evidence from multiple measures of performance. At the time, there was a double-digit gap between white and African American students, but one white teacher believed that "there's a small achievement gap in terms of race, but I think it mostly comes from a student's incoming background knowledge. From what I see, there are definitely high- and low-performing kids across all races." One African American teacher believed the problem was more about student and parent beliefs than teachers' expectations: "I don't think it's a racial thing. It's a clash between inner-city thinking and suburban expectations. Most of our African American students have left the inner cities and come to the suburbs because parents want to buy homes. They come to county schools where the environments are not predominantly black, and so they have to compete in a more rigid program. We're also struggling because of the lack of parent support. We often call home. Phone numbers are disconnected. You try to send a letter home, the child intercepts the letter and the parent never receives it."

A white teacher thought that the explicit focus on student subgroups actually contributed to the problem, saying, "I think there is racism in disguise. I think we like to say that we're color-blind, but the reality is we're continually targeting these children. Why don't we just say we're trying to raise achievement? Why do we have to preface it with race? I want all my students to succeed. I don't just want the minority students to succeed."

Graves was well aware of assumptions reflected in such comments:

> I think the central issue is that we don't want to talk about race. Most of us as white, mainstream Americans have been taught to be color-blind. So we assume that everybody's like us. And when we put interventions in place for a student of color based on our own white, middle-class perspectives, and the intervention doesn't work, we then unconsciously or sometimes consciously say, "Well see, we did this fabulous intervention and it didn't work. It must be the kids." It's not done in a malicious or intentional way, but it happens in classrooms every day. This is very difficult work because teachers tend to deny, defend, or shut down when you bring up issues of race. They've chosen this profession because they want to help children, but what is not understood is that despite our good intention, our teaching practices don't always have a positive impact on the student.

THE WORK ON THE GROUND

Even with the variability in individual beliefs and expectations, the district had made measurable progress in narrowing the achievement gap by 2005, mainly because there were so many successful experiments going on in schools. The executive team began identifying the schools that had performed ahead of the pack in order to understand what practices and behaviors school teams engaged in to produce results. Some of the early successes, such as Broad Acres and Viers Mill Elementary schools, were captured in written case studies that would later be used in the district's PLCI. Others, such as Piney Branch Elementary School and Westland Middle School, appeared in other publications. As the stories that follow demonstrate, the four used very different interventions to bring their students to high levels of academic achievement—not by accident. Operating in diverse communities with different students and staff, the schools had the freedom to differentiate their approaches. But there was a common thread running through all four examples—all of these school teams worked on implementing systems and processes that required their staffs to engage in behaviors that were consistent with the belief that all students can master high-level content, and that it is the role of the adults in schools to help them do just that. Some school staff obviously already shared these beliefs. In some instances, there is evidence that beliefs have come along as the new behaviors produced results for students. In others, the jury is still out.

Broad Acres Elementary School

In the spring of 2000, Broad Acres Elementary School was in serious trouble. With grade 3 proficiency at 13 percent in reading and 5 percent in mathematics, the state assessment results revealed yet another year of low student achievement. As one of the lowest-performing schools in the state, Broad Acres qualified for state-imposed restructuring. And if the school did not turn around and bring up student test scores, the state would take it over. With a poverty rate of 89 percent, the highest in MCPS, the school enrolled five hundred students from thirty-one countries, who spoke twenty-eight languages. Nearly 75 percent of the students did not speak English at home; most were from Africa, the Caribbean, and Central and South America.

The principal, Jody Leleck, hired in 1999, believed all students could succeed with the right support. She had been a teacher of English for

Speakers of Other Languages and a principal in MCPS since 1985, all in Title I schools. In her first year at Broad Acres, she attempted to work with teachers and staff to improve student performance, with little success. Following the release of the dismal math and reading test scores, the district came up with a restructuring plan for the school. Under Weast's direction, the planning involved the unions as well as key district departments: curriculum, organizational development, shared accountability, and human resources. The three unions all supported an agreement that required staff to make a three-year commitment to the school or to transfer out before the reform work began. As Leleck said:

> We came up with three action steps. One was people who wanted to remain here had to commit for three years. Two was that everyone had to take *The Skillful Teacher*. And the third was that people would work 15 extra days and be paid a stipend for that work. Dr. Weast was very clear that we would turn the school around using the resources we had. There was not going to be any more money—no extra funds, no extra resources, no extra staffing. Dr. Weast was wonderful and very honest—brutally honest. He said, 'if this fails, your career may be over here. Do you really want to do it? It's going to be tough.' After I made my commitment, I felt both empowered and supported by the district to make decisions that best suited Broad Acres.[2]

Over the next few years, the school was able to implement the plan. Practices included group work by teachers to look at student performance data; a reduction in class size; teacher reassignment; focused professional development and investments in individual teacher performance. The hard work paid off. In 2004 Broad Acres was removed from the state's watch list for underperforming schools. The remarkable performance gain—proficiency levels in grade 3 increasing from 13 percent to 75 percent in reading and from 5 percent to 67 percent in mathematics—highlights the success of the program.

Viers Mill Elementary School

Only the second Title I school in MCPS to earn the top state honor of Maryland Blue Ribbon School of Excellence, Viers Mill Elementary School used an innovative approach to put data in the hands of its students. At Viers Mill, a Red Zone school, 65 percent of students received a free or reduced-priced meal, 54 percent were Hispanic, 23 percent were African American, and one-third received ESOL services. Despite the demographics of the school, more than 90 percent of students in grade 3 achieved at or above proficiency in reading and math. Principal Jamie Virga attributed the success to teamwork and his talented staff, but it was also his careful hiring practices, thorough planning, and relentless focus on data that brought Viers Mill to such high levels of achievement.

Student performance data is thoroughly intertwined in the daily routine at Viers Mill. Teachers use formative assessments to monitor student progress and then modify their instructional approaches based on what they see in the data. There is also a strong culture among the teachers of sharing data and discovering new ways to analyze and display it. This has been key to changing the culture of expectations in the school. As one longtime teacher said, "We do look at data a lot more than we used to. We begin with the end in mind. We know what's expected and so (we) don't have an excuse."[3] Another teacher noted, "We really know our kids. We look at the data and talk as a team about what works well."[4] Finding new sources of data is also important. Building on the district strategy to have every student reading at proficiency by grade 3, the staff developed their own reading comprehension monitoring tool, which was a package of pre- and postformative assessments and reading samples aligned with MCPS curriculum and state standards. Teachers use the tool to track their students' reading levels quarterly on graphs that are then given to the students so they can chart their own progress. Students set goals, monitor and record their progress, and fully participate in data-driven decision making to increase their individual achievement. Students at Viers Mill have taken charge of their own development, working harder to become better readers.

Piney Branch Elementary School

At Piney Branch Elementary School, a grades 3–5 school with a 42 percent African American and 24 percent Hispanic student population, the leadership team was determined to offer more minority students access to Math A (sixth-grade-level math). For four years, the school's principal had directed third- and fourth-grade teachers to get more minority students ready for Math A by the end of fourth grade. In spring 2005, the leadership team evaluated students across seven fourth-grade sections, three of which were targeted for Math A. Teachers worried that a group of seventeen minority students would not be ready for success, so they created a separate class that would meet longer and more frequently to adequately meet the needs of the students. Their target was to double the number of Math A sections by the following year.

A staff member described why Piney Branch pushed so hard for more minority students in higher-level math: "We were two schools within one building—the majority school and the minority school. And in the last five years, we have been trying to build one community. Five years ago, the majority of white students would come from Takoma Park Elementary School coded GT (gifted and talented), and most of the minority kids had not qualified for GT. It took the right group of internal people with power who were ready to say, 'There's something wrong with this picture.' We had administrators who pushed hard for minority kids to go into advanced classes. And when you have that, things get moving."

Westland Middle School

Changes in behaviors were taking place in Green Zone schools, too, at Westland Middle School, an affluent school with a 64 percent white student population. Principal Ursula Hermann moved all eighth graders into English GT classes and eliminated the eighth grade on-level English curriculum. In her career working with low-income and minority students in rural and urban communities in Washington State, Ohio, and Virginia, she had seen plenty of examples of daily practices that reinforced inequities. She described the scenario at Westland that led to her decision: "We were developing the master schedule, and our assistant principal said, 'You know, we have 15 English sections, and 12 of them are for GT.' Since we had been observing a rise in what we refer to as 'de facto segregation' between on-level and GT classes, we looked at the demographics of on-level classes. What we discovered was that the composition of those classes was primarily our minority and special education students. So we just took a deep breath and said, 'We can't do this.'"

After reaching an agreement with Westland's cluster high school principal and the community superintendent, Hermann officially dissolved the on-level classes and reenrolled all students in GT English, which reassigned approximately five students to each class. She called parents and interviewed reassigned students to make them aware of the situation and to find out what the school could do to support them. Responding to remarks from students saying, "I'm not as smart as those kids, I can't read as fast, I can't keep up," the school provided access to additional classes and an after-school learning lab that could assist them with English and writing. Hermann noted, "We had no more failures than we did when kids were in on-level classes. The kids rose to the occasion." Still, school administrators and teachers received pushback from a few parents who felt that the GT English courses had become less challenging. In one reported incident, parents questioned the rigor of the class because of the increased number of minorities in their children's class. Hermann reflected on the parent reactions, saying, "These concerns may have been fueled by stereotypical thinking or by a simple fear of change. They do want equity, but they also want to ensure their kids are challenged. I agree with them—we want all of our kids challenged. What I've done in eighth-grade English I haven't done in grades six and seven or in math, because the issue is so big. If I want my whole community to buy into it, I have to get them to truly understand that we are responsible for doing this with all students."

In fact, this was the challenge that the entire district faced in 2005. An African American principal in a successful Red Zone school described it this way: "As 'Jerry's kids' move up, they're going to encounter environments that won't be as receptive. I'm not saying that we're there yet as a school, but we're aware of where the challenges are. But I often wonder how our students will be received when they move on to other schools in the district. You can't change a school system until there are principals and people in place that have the same belief system and the right repertoire of skills. That's where we're stuck right now. The hard part is, how do you move people to the core beliefs that [they need]?"

With concrete examples of schools that had broken the link between race and achievement by implementing activities that required staff members to change their behaviors in ways that were consistent with beliefs about equity, the executive team members began thinking about ways that they could use these proof points to convince people all over the district that, contrary to what their personal beliefs might be, it was possible to engage in professional behaviors that would dramatically improve student learning. The evidence from their top-performing Red Zone schools suggested that if teachers saw results for students from the new behaviors, their beliefs would follow. The challenge was to go deeper in all of the Red Zone schools as well as in the Green Zone schools, most of which had some number of African American and Hispanic students.

PUTTING RACE ON THE TABLE

In the summer of 2005, the executive team members again participated in the Public Education Leadership Project (PELP). While sharing their differentiation strategy and the results it had produced with colleagues from other districts, they began to think seriously about what challenges remained to achieving excellence and equity across the entire system. As a team, they committed to working intensely on this question when they returned to Montgomery County. In the early weeks following the retreat, senior administrators debated the appropriate language to use when discussing race issues within the district. While some preferred the description *removing institutional barriers*, others favored the term *institutionalized racism* because they believed that it most accurately described the real issue. A few administrators expressed concerns that using the word *racism* could potentially spark fear in some administrators and teachers who would misinterpret it to mean that they were racist. Weast distinguished between the two phrases, explaining that "institutionalized racism is the failure to act on removing institutional barriers that hold students of a particular race behind." The team decided to explicitly define *institutional barriers* as those policies, procedures, and practices that do not serve all children equitably.

As they were developing ideas about how to communicate this to principals at the annual back-to-school leadership conference, Hurricane Katrina hit New Orleans. The images Weast saw from the disaster reaffirmed his commitment to eliminating the achievement gap in MCPS. Katrina became a rallying cry for Weast as he addressed principals and administrators at the leadership conference: "That hurricane did something to me . . . you and I have talked about raise the bar and close the gap, and I've talked about who gets left behind if we don't have education. And I've actually been overemotional on this many times. But you know, the one thing that struck me was how people were sorted. It just really got to me. I know it got to you and other people. I can [usually] close my eyes and see the beautiful mountains when I feel troubled. Now when I close my eyes, I see those folks huddled in the Superdome with the roof coming off or in that facility in Houston. It's hard to say it's not about race, isn't it?"[5] Later in his talk, he declared, "Now I am going to get right down into the race issue, and I am going to talk about *Hispanic* and *African American*. And if it hurts, I'm sorry. I apologize respectfully, but I am going to talk about it. You need to talk about it. You need to have that [conversation] because we are going to [work] together to destroy institutional barriers that have sorted kids for way too long." He ended by flatly stating, "We're not going to wake up one morning and find that our kids can't get out of town because they don't have enough money or any access [to public services]."[6]

Because they drew on a current event that was part of the national dialogue, his remarks galvanized the assembled leadership group by giving them a concrete picture of the outcomes that result from institutional barriers and sorting mechanisms that reinforce social inequities. The executive leadership team faced a formidable task to develop concrete ways to put people's best intentions into action.

IMPLEMENTING A MULTIFACETED APPROACH

As we described in chapter 5, one way that community superintendents, other central office leaders, and principals responded to Weast's charge was by setting a target for minority PSAT participation and taking M-STAT a step further through the development of the Honors/AP Potential Identification Tool (HAPIT). Not satisfied with the rate of progress being made, deputy superintendent Frieda Lacey even started meeting one-on-one with students who had been flagged by HAPIT but not placed in an honors or AP course. Lacey also helped create school-monitoring calendars to bring consistency across the community superintendents. The calendars established specific pieces of data that each level—elementary, middle, and high—would focus on for the month. For example, in December all high schools were to collect and analyze the following data points:

- Number and percentage of students taking the PSAT

- Number of students with high absenteeism

- Number and percentage of students suspended; number of students with multiple suspensions

- Number and percentage of students not on target to complete geometry by the end of grade 10

- Number and percentage of students participating in the November SAT; overall student performance on the exam

- Number and percentage of students enrolled in rigorous courses; number of students who can be moved to more rigorous instruction

In addition, specific school improvement benchmarks for minority students were established through 2010. Previously, metrics were set systemwide; now, individual schools were responsible for instituting annual targets for each racial subgroup. To further engage parents and schools in dialogues about race, MCPS created diverse school community discussion groups called Study Circles. Based on a nationally recognized model, the Study Circles program brought together groups of parents, teachers, and students from school communities to address racial and ethnic barriers impacting student achievement. The groups meet weekly for six two-hour sessions and typically consist of fifteen parents, several school staff members, and students, where appropriate. In 2006–2007, twenty-three Study Circles met throughout the district, with participants closely reflecting the demographics of their schools: 29 percent African American, 8 percent Asian American, 26 percent Hispanic, and 33 percent white.

The MCPS team believes the Study Circles have brought a deeper understanding about racial differences to the community and serve as a catalyst for problem solving in each school. This belief is born out by recent evaluation data. Nearly 90 percent of participants—both parents and staff—reported an increase in their understanding of others' attitudes and beliefs. As one principal reflected, "When you hear some of these experiences, all other differences kind of melt away. The Study Circle helped make people stronger to deal with the issues."[7] A parent added, "I think it made teachers and parents who participated more aware of . . . racial issues that we didn't know we had. And it set us on the path to deal with those issues. Also it helped us to think about not being so complacent about kids, minority kids who are not being successful. Instead of kind of nudging them, we're going to be pushing them . . . and not waiting until something desperate happens, but starting now."[8]

As the Study Circles helped MCPS become more proactive about addressing the achievement gap among community members, Weast was growing more concerned about the lack of diversity in leadership positions in the district. To boost the numbers of minorities, especially Hispanics, in administrative positions, Weast formed the Minority Leadership Recruitment Committee. The committee reached out to principals and community members for nominations of minorities for school leadership positions, gathering the names of 108 African American, 18 Asian, 20 Hispanic, and 20 other ethnic candidates. MCPS then invited the nominees to a Future Administrators Workshop to "tap them on the shoulder" and further develop their interest as well as provide a networking forum with executive leadership. Principals were asked to provide leadership opportunities to these prospective candidates in order to build their skills and experiences to become administrators.

During this time, the district also developed a system for spreading effective practices that emerged from M-STAT meetings. In August 2007, it created a *PSAT M-STAT Data Booklet* detailing effective strategies to increase PSAT participation. Several months later, it did the same for SAT participation and honors/AP enrollment. The guides were then used to train school teams in professional development sessions in February. It appeared that the hard work was paying off. In 2007, more than 90 percent of kindergartners finished their year reading at grade level, regardless of race or income. Nearly 60 percent of African American high school students took at least one advanced placement course, increasing from around 30 percent in 1999. This compared to only 13 percent of African American students in the state of Maryland and 5 percent nationwide. MCPS had the highest number of African American AP exam takers scoring well enough to earn college credit of any district in the nation save for New York City, which has nine times more African American students.

Nevertheless, much work remained. Performance on AP exams had not accelerated at the same pace as enrollment and exam taking, but it had not declined either. Though the barriers to AP entry had been dramatically lowered, MCPS needed to ensure that all students were prepared to excel, not just participate, in rigorous courses. Even so, five times more African American and two times as many Hispanic students in MCPS scored a 3 or higher on AP tests, as compared to their respective groups nationwide. Furthermore, PSAT participation districtwide was at 91.7 percent, with 88.1 percent of African American and 84.4 percent of Hispanic grade 10 students taking the exam. Nevertheless, in the 2007–2008 school year, there were still seven schools not meeting PSAT targets in four or five subgroups. More work needed to be done.

As conversations about the achievement gap became more commonplace and MCPS created new and more refined tools for dealing with the problem, Weast and his team noticed a shift in the tone of conversations occurring throughout the district. While there was an undercurrent of respect for diversity, district staff and parents' discussions became more and more about equity of opportunities. In one particular meeting within the Office of Organizational Development, a phrase was mentioned that slowly began to work its way through MCPS: "Let us aspire to create a school system where student achievement is no longer predictable by race."

Intrigued by the idea of a completely equitable district, Weast sent a new team that included a community superintendent and a principal to the Public Education Leadership Project in July 2008. Their challenge from Weast was complex but straightforward—come back with a definition of an equitable school district: a list of things you would look for to assess whether or not MCPS was meeting that standard. Weast believed that if MCPS was going to take the next step in addressing the achievement gap, it would have to move from looking at the problem from the perspective of diversity and adopt the language and practices of equity.

In order to get started, the team reflected on MCPS's past work by looking at data. Team members saw that while the aggregate numbers showed that dramatic progress had been made, a disproportionate share of the improvement had happened at "islands of excellence"— individual schools where disparities in achievement between races had been nearly eliminated. There were still plenty of schools with larger-than-average gaps, indicating that perhaps these teams had not fully embraced the behaviors necessary for breaking the link between race and outcomes.

The team's analysis also led the members to observe that many of MCPS's initiatives were reactive in nature. HAPIT was created only after the executive team observed a major problem in PSAT participation and honors/AP enrollment. The team acknowledged the difficult road ahead and began to brainstorm characteristics of the equitable school district MCPS aspired to be and to think about what it would take to build systems that were more proactive.

Returning to MCPS, board of education president Nancy Navarro asked the PELP team to continue its work throughout the school year. A few additional members were added to the team, including Donna Graves. The team's work started building on the new dialogue in MCPS around the idea of equity (as opposed to diversity), but people still weren't sure how to convert their conversations into action.

In an early-fall meeting, they had a breakthrough. Glenn Singleton, whose work on *Courageous Conversations* had long been part of diversity training, had agreed to consult directly with MCPS on its efforts to explicitly address race and achievement. During a meeting, he noticed the frameworks, process diagrams, and data maps that adorned the conference room walls, and asked why it was that they had not developed an equity framework for the district. Such a tool could be adapted to help every employee in the district understand what equitable practices would look like in their work and how those might ultimately connect with student learning.

The question sparked a renewed intensity to break the links between race and student outcomes. MCPS added an equity section to its teacher observation forms that would look for evidence of equitable instructional practices. The monthly administrators and supervisors (A&S) meetings also became completely focused on promoting equity and eliminating achievement gaps. In the first meeting in September 2008, principals divided into clusters and looked at their K–12 student achievement disaggregated by race. People in each cluster asked themselves the same question: how are we doing? Although some community superintendents had looked at K–12 data for their entire cluster with their principals, others had only worked at the individual school level through the M-STAT process. By building cluster-level analysis into its A&S meeting, MCPS was sending the signal that this kind of analysis and conversation was necessary if the district were going to make sure that the entire K–12 value chain was arranged for equity. So that there was no confusion, Weast explicitly told the group before they broke up into clusters, "This works needs to be done, must be done, and you are the only ones who can do it. You need to do it. I know you are going to do it."[9]

In concert with the renewed focus on breaking the link between race and achievement, the district revised its Pathway to Success to reflect the newest thinking about what steps in the K–12 chain would signal progress toward graduating ready for college. Named the Seven Keys to College Readiness (see figure 6.1), the new path increased the rigor at a number of grade levels and added new benchmarks based on analysis of years of data that revealed correlations between early-grade performance and later achievement.

Graves reflected on why this districtwide renewal for equity and excellence was important, saying, "Most are still in diversity training

FIG. 6.1 **Seven keys to college readiness**

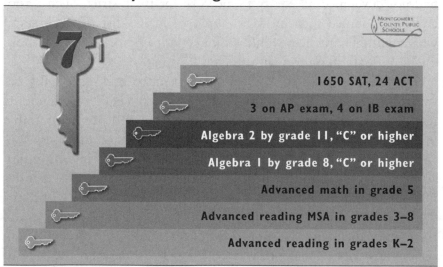

1650 SAT, 24 ACT

3 on AP exam, 4 on IB exam

Algebra 2 by grade 11, "C" or higher

Algebra 1 by grade 8, "C" or higher

Advanced math in grade 5

Advanced reading MSA in grades 3–8

Advanced reading in grades K–2

Source: Montgomery County Public Schools.

mode, where you can use the word *diversity* to cover a lot of things and not have to say *race*. Back when there was a gender gap, no one was afraid to say *boy* or *girl*. But no one wants to say *white* and *black*. We were taught to be color-blind. For people to understand that we are part of the problem is painful. That is hard for people. We've been talking about race, expectations, and teacher efficacy. Those unsurfaced biases and prejudices lead to a decrease in expectations for black and brown kids. We have to be honest about that and be willing to say it out loud."[10]

Many principals appeared to be up to the challenge of the enormous undertaking. The renamed Equity Training and Development Department saw requests for its services go from five schools in 2005, to fourteen in 2006, to thirty in 2007, and to seventy-two in the first few months of 2008. Two additional specialists were hired to handle the increased demand, and the group started to train schools on topics such as critical race theory. Though there was still a long way to go, Graves noted, "Now we have to build a systemic plan to address what no other large school district has done. A systemic equity plan has to happen by building the capacity of a leadership group in each workplace. We have to develop groups that can lead for equity in an informal way in schools and workplaces. We have to build the critical mass of awareness and leadership in each building."[11]

The team working on the equity framework is continuing to develop its elements through subcommittee work. The members planned to finish a draft by December 2008 and begin a vetting process with stakeholder groups before sharing it during the A&S meeting in February 2009. After incorporating feedback from these groups, they hope the new equity framework will become district policy before the end of the academic year, around the time this book hits the shelves.

The next chapter reflects on the work at MCPS since 1999 and proposes some lessons learned from its journey.

CHAPTER SEVEN

Six Lessons from the Montgomery County Journey and a New Call to Action

[This] is an inspiring story because of the commitment of the people in Montgomery County to be relentless in their pursuit of excellence for every student . . . [E]very year tens of thousands of students have a chance to beat the odds that are stacked against minority and low-income children in this country.

The Montgomery County Public Schools have been on a ten-year journey to create a twenty-first-century school district that provides all of its students with access to an excellent education. They have made dramatic progress, but as we noted at the end of chapter 6, much work remains.

One way to think about the MCPS work is by "action areas," which is how we organized the chapters. This framing answers the question "What did they do?" They developed a strategy, invested in people, designed systems, and so forth. This can be a helpful way of making sense of the complex set of interdependent decisions and activities that took place over time.

But another question is, "Why did they get results?" MCPS is just one district, situated in a particular context; nevertheless, six lessons from its work are relevant to other district, school, and community leaders. For district and school leaders interested in adopting a process for analyzing their own performance problems and developing and implementing strategies for improvement in a way that is similar to the MCPS approach, the next chapter will provide a framework that a number of large districts have found helpful. But first, the six lessons:

1. Implementing a strategy of common, rigorous standards with differentiated resources and instruction can create excellence and equity for all students.

2. Adopting a "value chain" approach to the K–12 continuum increases quality and provides a logical frame for strategic choices.

3. Blurring the lines between governance, management, staff, and community increases capacity and accountability.

4. Creating systems and structures that change behaviors is a way to shift beliefs if they lead to student learning gains.

5. Breaking the link between race, ethnicity, and student outcomes is difficult without confronting the effect that beliefs about race and ethnicity have on student learning.

6. Leading for equity matters.

These six lessons cut across the various action areas and are present in many of the initiatives we have discussed. For each lesson, examples from earlier in the book and a few new ones will help to illuminate the insights.

LESSON 1: IMPLEMENTING A STRATEGY OF COMMON, RIGOROUS STANDARDS WITH DIFFERENTIATED RESOURCES AND INSTRUCTION CAN CREATE EXCELLENCE AND EQUITY FOR ALL STUDENTS

When the MCPS community agreed to college and work readiness for all students as its North Star in *Our Call to Action*, the stage was set for the development of rigorous standards that were more challenging than the state of Maryland's proficiency standards. State standards often serve as a minimum level of acceptable performance, not an ambitious statement about the potential of all students to achieve at high levels. By aligning the district's curriculum framework to aggressive targets consistent with preparation for college and high-wage work, the leaders at MCPS created a common standard of excellence that would apply to every classroom in every school.

The big idea behind the differentiation strategy was that equity ≠ equal. The strategy had two components: resources and instruction. The Red Zone/Green Zone approach was a clear way to communicate how resources would flow differentially to MCPS schools based on what they needed to provide equitable learning opportunities to their students. If students were far behind relative to the rigorous common standards, they would need more time to catch up, and time costs money. While it was impossible to add more hours to the day (except in the case of full-day kindergarten), Red Zone schools could "buy time" through having staff development teachers in every school and technological supports that freed up teachers from administrative tasks and helped them better diagnose student learning needs so that they could spend more time on instructional activities that were likely to improve learning. And because quality in the Green Zone never wavered, the social compact to invest more in the Red Zone remained intact as those investments produced returns in the form of accelerated progress.

The other component of the differentiation strategy was instruction. Sometimes when educators hear terms such as *common standards* and *aligned curriculum*, they imagine that their creativity and professional judgment are about to be overrun with scripts and lock-step teaching plans. At MCPS, this was not the case. While it is true that the school board created a policy that required teachers to deliver the common curriculum, the strategy to improve performance was premised on the assumption that students with different learning needs required different levels of resources and varied instructional approaches.

Effective differentiation of instruction requires diagnosing student needs, developing potential solutions, putting them into practice, and reflecting on their effectiveness. This is a professional endeavor, not a technical task. The strategy of differentiation respects and elevates teachers' roles as critical to the learning of all of their students.

As we saw in several instances earlier in the book, principals used a variety of tactics to accelerate the learning of African American and Hispanic students, including abolishing on-grade-level courses and putting data in students' hands. Innovations such as these were not simply tolerated but encouraged by the executive team. As the work became more sophisticated, M-STAT provided a forum for sharing practices that worked, gathering them into guidebooks and distributing them to other school communities—not as mandatory practices, but as examples of things that had produced results for students.

In the end, the strategy in MCPS was based on the assumption that every single child is capable of meeting rigorous standards, but each child starts from a different place. Because of residential patterns, students who were farthest behind were concentrated in certain areas, allowing for increased, differential investments at the school level based on students' learning needs. In the same way that teachers were asked to differentiate their work based on the needs of their students, the district strategy was to differentiate resources and support based on the needs of schools and teachers.

LESSON 2: ADOPTING A "VALUE CHAIN" APPROACH TO THE K–12 CONTINUUM INCREASES QUALITY AND PROVIDES A LOGICAL FRAME FOR STRATEGIC CHOICES

Throughout the book, we have explored a number of ways in which the MCPS team used a K-through-12 lens to make decisions about standards, curriculum, and instruction. One way to describe this aspect of their work is a "value chain" approach. Adapted from management thinking, a *value chain* is simply a chain of activities, each of which adds some value to the eventual outcome. The sum of the value at the end of chain is more than the sum of the added values of all activities. In this context, the well-worn phrase "The whole is greater than the sum of its parts" applies. Because the activities along the chain are by nature interdependent, backward mapping from the desired end state through each link to the beginning of the chain to determine what must happen at each stage has a compelling logic.

This kind of thinking shows up throughout Montgomery County's story. By setting its North Star as college and work readiness, the district could point to existing indicators of progress toward the standard. SAT scores were highly correlated with college success, AP courses were highly correlated with SAT success, and PSAT scores were highly correlated with AP course success. Hence, the intense focus on PSAT participation for minority students. Algebra by eighth grade was another predictor of AP math enrollment and success, and this drove the development of the Mathematics Pathway, charting the course from elementary school math classes all the way through high school.

Of course, creating the overall district standards and curricular framework was an extended backward-mapping exercise. Each step along the way in any content area from the early grades through high school has been deeply examined and operationalized in the common MCPS curriculum, with each piece designed to deliver students to the next grade prepared for success, eventually reaching Algebra 2 and AP courses by eleventh grade, and 1650 on the SAT by twelfth grade.

The district's development and use of increasingly sophisticated data and forecasting tools fits within this concept as well. As described in chapter 5, the research department discovered which kindergarten reading text level is most correlated with third-grade success, prompting the executive team and school leaders to reconsider the benchmark for kindergarten success. This is the kind of value chain orientation that produces results for students.

Individual schools also use this thinking when they use their time in creative ways. For example, at Wayside Elementary School (K–5), principal Yong Mi Kim and her staff conceive of their time with children not grade by grade, but as a six-year time horizon. This allows them to adjust the curriculum to work across grade levels. Some second graders can be in a math section with an overlap between the second- and third-grade curricula, while some of their second-grade classmates are in a blended third- and fourth-grade section. This practice supports moving students by more than one grade level in a single year. For Wayside and many other schools in MCPS, success is not finishing second grade on level, but finishing it ready for success in third grade and beyond, regardless of where a student started the year.

Another benefit of value chain thinking is that it allows leaders to identify key leverage points in the chain, which helps inform decisions about sequence and pace. Because of capacity constraints, it is nearly impossible to do everything at once. Thinking K through 12 means that MCPS could focus at first on early-grade reading and bookend it with a focus on access to high school honors and AP courses—and still generate results throughout the system. Next up was eighth-grade algebra, requiring decisions about fourth- and fifth-grade math. The value chain approach helps frame the logic of choices about sequence and speed so that district leaders can better communicate to internal and external stakeholders how their actions are likely to lead to results.

LESSON 3: BLURRING THE LINES BETWEEN GOVERNANCE, MANAGEMENT, STAFF, AND COMMUNITY INCREASES CAPACITY AND ACCOUNTABILITY

When leaders think of their organizational capacity as limited to the people who work for them, they are prone to engage in a set of suboptimal, if rational, behaviors. The board becomes a body to be kept at arm's length and given just enough information to keep it out of the staff's way. Union officials are seen as parties in opposition to be cajoled and outmaneuvered, and at times bargained into submission. Parents and other community members might be honored with the language of *customer* and *partner* but treated as an obligation (or irritation). Weast made a different choice early in his tenure at MCPS and has backed it up with ten years of actions that have promoted his notion of *shared accountability*. By blurring the lines between the traditional boxes—boards govern, managers decide, staff implements, and families and communities benefit—Weast created the conditions under which multiple stakeholder groups felt as if they owned the results. But this method also dramatically expanded the district's capacity to analyze problems and develop and implement solutions, because committed and highly skilled people from all of those groups populated the committees, task forces, and advisory groups that were engaged in the hard work of planning the implementation of the differentiation strategy.

It is important to recognize that the healthy working relationship among all of these groups was not inevitable. When Weast arrived, board members rarely agreed and barely spoke to each other; the three unions were at odds with each other and the district; and Red Zone and Green Zone parents might as well have been in different districts. Weast's willingness to blur the lines rather than consolidate power to himself and his employees was a first step, and leaders and members of all of these groups have reciprocated by deeply engaging in the important work of achieving excellence and equity for all MCPS students. The groups still have their individual interests and obligations to fulfill their formal duties, which naturally lead to tensions and disagreements, but by and large most difficulties are resolved with an eye toward the groups' mutually agreed-on vision of what is best for student learning. As *Leading for Equity* went to press in March 2009, the employee unions received national attention for their commitment to the strategy. In his *New York Times* column about the public outrage over executive bonuses at troubled American International Group (AIG), Tom Friedman wrote of the teachers in Montgomery County: "I live in Montgomery County, MD. The schoolteachers here, who make on average $67,000 a year, recently voted to voluntarily give up their 5 percent pay raise that was *contractually* agreed to for next year, saving our school system $89 million—so programs and teachers would not have to be terminated. If public schoolteachers can take one for schoolchildren and fellow teachers, AIG brokers can take one for the country."[1] Though the column only mentions teachers, the $89 million actually came from all unionized employees in the district when they voted overwhelmingly in favor of a proposal from their union leaders in response to a budget forecast that put at risk ongoing investments in the strategy that they had helped create. Weast described the unions' actions with a saying he attributes to his father: "When people help build the barn, they are less likely to set it on fire."[2]

MCPS is also working to blur the lines between classrooms and schools. By creating an environment in which teachers are expected to work together on schoolwide performance issues, the district is trying to solve the problem of isolation that plagues the teaching profession. Teaching and learning problems are often widely shared, but the solutions are widely distributed in the heads and hands of teachers who are working on their own every day to accelerate their students' learning. By blurring the lines between classrooms, and even grade levels, MCPS is more rapidly diffusing knowledge about what works. The same is true for principals. Creating mechanisms for sharing what works, such as M-STAT, helps blur the boundaries between schools so that the district's capacity to improve increases at a faster rate.

LESSON 4: CREATING SYSTEMS AND STRUCTURES THAT CHANGE BEHAVIORS IS A WAY TO SHIFT BELIEFS AND LEADS TO STUDENT LEARNING GAINS

Educators talk frequently about school culture and its importance for learning. These conversations are usually about how to change a dysfunctional culture so that it better serves students. In some ways, it is the holy grail: "If only we could change the culture of schooling, then we could . . ." Culture is simply the aggregate beliefs and behaviors of the people in an organization, whether a school, a department, or a district. So to change a culture, where should one start? Beliefs? Behaviors? MCPS struggled with this early on. The team's communication and messaging efforts attempted to signal the organizational beliefs that would lead to breaking the link between race, class, and achievement. Beliefs such as high expectations, effort-based intelligence, and a relentless focus on using data to help students meet standards were reinforced in meetings and memos. But how might people who don't already share those beliefs change quickly enough to rapidly increase student performance?

The answer for MCPS was to focus on concrete systems and structures that made it necessary for people to engage in behaviors consistent with the beliefs. For instance, common grading and reporting is a system that puts into action the belief that all students should be held to high standards, regardless of their race or family income. The mCLASS:Reading 3D tool requires teachers to behave in ways consistent with beliefs about effort-based intelligence and using data. M-STAT is a system that ties together data use all over the district into a common format that forces people to engage in behaviors that reflect the belief that institutional barriers exist and can be removed. Adding equitable practices indicators to teacher evaluations reinforces actions that are rooted in beliefs about the link between expectations and learning. When these behaviors produce results, there is evidence in MCPS that for many (but perhaps not all), beliefs will follow. Weast reflected on this idea, saying, "I thought I would enter the change process through the culture door and then engage everyone in creating systems and structures that would support the culture. But I couldn't get traction, so we started to build the systems anyway, and it seemed that the culture started to shift as people saw that the changes worked for kids."[3] As we saw in chapter 6, MCPS still has work to do on this front, and the push to develop a new equity framework that explicitly defines equitable practices for every role in the district is an attempt to accelerate the culture change necessary to create a district that produces excellence and equity for every student.

LESSON 5: BREAKING THE LINK BETWEEN RACE, ETHNICITY, AND STUDENT OUTCOMES IS DIFFICULT WITHOUT CONFRONTING THE EFFECT THAT BELIEFS ABOUT RACE AND ETHNICITY HAVE ON STUDENT LEARNING

In chapter 1, we pointed out that in the early 1990s, MCPS superintendent Paul Vance and his team created a strategic plan with explicit references to minority students and the gap between subgroups. The board would approve the plan only if the team downplayed the language. For the rest of that decade, the district made no demonstrable progress on narrowing achievement gaps. In 1999, *Our Call to Action* had specific language about racial and ethnic groups, but by and large Weast and his team understandably crafted phrases that were more subtle, such as *raise the bar, close the gap* and *Red Zone/Green Zone*. This helped build early agreement and momentum for a controversial new strategy that proposed to invest differentially in the learning of African American and Hispanic students.

While some on the executive leadership team and many Red Zone school teams discussed race and ethnicity in their planning and data analysis, the broader district and public communications in the early days were less pointed. This approach allowed the strategy to gather steam and produce results for students. But as the work progressed, the institutional barriers that were largely invisible to the community and many district and school staff could no longer be ignored if MCPS were to achieve the lofty goals of *Our Call to Action*. Discussing barriers to performance in terms of race became imperative if they were to create a district in which all students had access to rigorous content.

In chapter 6, we saw that as the executive leadership team was wrestling with how to "put race on the table" in 2005, Hurricane Katrina devastated New Orleans. This provided a moment for Weast to say to every principal and central office leader at one time, "I'm going to get right down into the race issue . . . *Hispanic* and *African American* . . . and you need to talk about it."[4] The speech marked a shift in the intensity and transparency with which race and ethnicity became required topics of discussion, analysis, and planning. The fact that race is a difficult topic in society at large permeates efforts to discuss it productively in schools, creating an ironic situation in which we aim to solve racial achievement gaps without ever talking explicitly about race. The Donna Graves quote in chapter 6 about the gender gap is instructive; three decades ago, educators were not uncomfortable using the words *boy* and *girl* in tackling the root causes of that gap, but using the words *black* and *white* in trying to understand and solve predictable differences among racial subgroups is another story.

The MCPS community has taken on the challenge of creating an environment in which people are expected to discuss race and achievement, including the impact that beliefs about race have on expectations and student learning. In addition to diversity training and study circles, systems like M-STAT and HAPIT explicitly focus on racial and ethnic indicators, and provide forums and protocols for people to discuss them productively with an eye toward building the capacity of individuals and teams to analyze the performance problems and examine the degree to which their own behaviors and the beliefs reflected in the structures of their organization actually contribute to the problems.

The MCPS team believes that this deeper focus will accelerate its efforts to break the link between race and achievement. The team's current vision statement makes a bold claim about its intentions: "Let us aspire to create a school system where achievement is no longer predictable by race."

LESSON 6: LEADING FOR EQUITY MATTERS

When we began writing this book, we set a benchmark for ourselves. If readers finished the last chapter and their answer to the question of how to apply the lessons from MCPS was simply "Hire Jerry Weast," then we would have failed. So many times, the stories of reform journeys in large districts hinge on the exploits of a noble hero, Dr. Superintendent. Our aim has been to briefly highlight many of the leaders around the system who created the results in MCPS, while understanding that we could never introduce them all. More importantly, we wanted to provide some concrete examples of what they did and why it worked (or did not). We hope that we have approached that benchmark.

However, it is impossible to understand the MCPS story without recognizing the enormous impact that leading for equity has had on the children of Montgomery County. Jerry Weast was attracted to MCPS because he believed that the board was sincere in its desire to tackle the achievement gap and that the county had the resources to do it. From the beginning, he envisioned his leadership task as mobilizing the community to create excellence and equity for all students. His entire strategy was focused on this aim, and he has never wavered. This is not to say that he has not made mistakes, for he surely has. But his focus on building the capacity of people in the system to effectively deliver a high-quality education to every single child in the district has been constant. And for a decade, in public and in private, he has consistently made the case that giving all students access to rigorous content is the right thing to do morally and the smart thing to do economically.

Some of his public interactions cause discomfort, sometimes intentionally. We have discussed the Katrina speech, but there are other examples. For instance, during the kindergarten wars, a Green Zone father shouted out during a board meeting, "Why can't my child have full-day kindergarten?" Weast's response? "He can if you move to the Red Zone." These kinds of moments are seared into the collective conscience of people in MCPS because they reinforced his commitment to the strategy and galvanized the team to stand firm in the face of criticism. One of his greatest contributions was deliberately modeling what it meant to lead for equity.

Many board members, union officials, school teams, and central office staff also engaged in leadership for equity. In chapter 3, we saw a dysfunctional board recommit to a focus on equitable student learning, and then stand by that commitment for ten years—no easy task for a revolving group of elected officials. Two-time board president Nancy Navarro was a driving force in the creation of the multistakeholder team crafting the new equity framework and is herself a member. She leads not only as a board member, but as a parent. Her children attend Red Zone schools.

In chapters 3 and 4, we saw leadership from union officials Bonnie Cullison, Rebecca Newman, and Merle Cuttitta, who were willing not only to participate fully in the development of a strategy for equity, but to take the lead in crafting an effective process for removing underperforming staff so that the district's capacity to implement effectively would grow even faster.

When deputy superintendent Frieda Lacey and chief school performance officer Steve Bedford decided to create M-STAT and focus entirely on data about African American and Hispanic students, their leadership accelerated the entire district's focus on race as a substantive challenge that deserved the same level of analysis and planning that had become a hallmark of MCPS. When Lacey appeared in principals' offices with a list of names of qualified African American students in their buildings who were not in AP courses, and talked with students themselves about why they were not enrolling, she was leading for equity.

At Piney Branch Elementary, we heard a teacher say that the enrollment of minority students in higher-level math happened because "the right group of internal people with power were ready to say, 'There's something wrong with this picture,'" when the data showed that the advanced courses were filled with white students and the grade-level courses were filled with minority students. This is what we mean by leading for equity.

And this leadership must be broad based. In chapter 6, we saw the dramatic turnaround of Broad Acres under the leadership of Jody Leleck. Now that Leleck is the chief academic officer of MCPS, how is the school doing? The improvement has accelerated under the current teaching staff and new principal Michael Bayewitz, a longtime teacher in the district and former principal of Luxmanor Elementary. On the 2008 state tests, 90 percent of Broad Acres students were proficient or advanced in mathematics and 81 percent were proficient or advanced in reading. Broad Acres' student population is more than 90 percent minority and low income, with the highest poverty rate of the district's 199 schools. Its success provides proof that all students can meet or exceed standards and that no one person is the key to success. Leading for equity matters.

A NEW CALL TO ACTION

Leading for Equity is an inspiring story because of the commitment of the people in Montgomery County to be relentless in their pursuit of excellence for every student. As they aspire to create a school system where achievement is no longer predicable by race, every year tens of thousands of students have a chance to beat the odds that are stacked against minority and low-income children in this country. What would it take for that number to become hundreds of thousands, even millions, so that the odds change entirely?

First, in cities and counties all over the country, school board leaders, union officials, superintendents, teachers, principals, and other staff would have to join with parents and community leaders in a new call to action, just as they did in Montgomery County in 1999. By focusing first on what is best for student learning, even if it conflicts with existing adult interests, our schools would begin to make rapid progress. Whether it is committing to differential resources based on equity, not equality, agreeing to evaluation systems that identify and remove underperforming teachers, or disrupting entrenched patterns of tracking and sorting, adults could make a dramatic difference in the lives of young people in their communities. These actions would not completely break the link between race, income, and achievement, but they would be a significant start down the path. The ten-year coalition among the groups in Montgomery County is unique, but it is not impossible to replicate. The people there are like people everywhere; the difference is, they have been willing to continue to dig deeper and deeper into the root causes of the inequities in their county and face hard truths when they emerged without resorting to finger-pointing. The community at large believes it is *their* responsibility to ensure excellence and equity, not someone else's.

Money has been important to the success in Montgomery County, and it is true that the district is well resourced. But according to the National Center for Education Statistics, at $12,000 per student in 2005, MCPS was in the same range as many other large East Coast districts with similar cost structures, such as Washington, D.C. ($13,000), and New York City ($13,500), and much lower than Boston ($16,000) and Newark, New Jersey ($20,000). These urban districts have much higher percentages of minority and low-income students than Montgomery County overall but are very similar to some of the schools we saw in the Red Zone. Our only point here is that the lessons about what worked for schools in the Red Zone are worth consideration in urban districts and could potentially be paid for with a reallocation of dollars away from things that clearly do not work to interventions that are getting results. The politics in the larger urban districts are difficult, but so, too, were they in Montgomery County ten years ago.

It's important to remember that the MCPS strategy had two parts. Differentiation of resources and instruction, yes. But differentiation alone was not likely to create excellence. Common, rigorous standards were necessary to ensure that the equity the district was striving to create was about excellence. By setting North Star as readiness for college and high-wage work, MCPS converted the Maryland state tests into one of several important indicators of success. For districts in states with less rigorous standards than Maryland's, this is absolutely essential. Communities must not settle for the future that low or mediocre state standards envision for their children. As MCPS has done, so must other districts set college readiness as the goal and use external benchmarks to monitor their effectiveness at preparing students for compelling opportunities beyond high school.

The federal government should play a role here. Unlike most other developed countries, the United States does not have a set of national academic standards for student learning. By contrast, we do have common standards in almost all other important areas of public and private life. For example, we do not leave it to each state to create standards for college entrance exams; rather, we have national benchmarks for these important educational activities. We have national standards for health care, from medical procedures to prescription drugs, not fifty sets of state standards for this complicated and important endeavor. In fact, there are standards for just about everything we use or do on a daily basis. So it is not surprising that most Americans who are not deeply involved in the education sector assume that the country already has national standards outlining what each student should learn in order to graduate. After all, isn't that what all the fuss regarding No Child Left Behind was about?

When NCLB was signed into law in 2001, many states had already developed standards for their local school districts, but many had not. As the saying goes, Republicans don't like "national" and Democrats don't like "standards," so in order to get the bill passed, its sponsors did not propose a set of national standards, but rather directed each state to come up with its own. Each state also developed its own tests to assess student mastery of the standards, and the law threatened draconian intervention by state education departments on behalf of the federal government and loss of Title I funding if targets were not met. This created incentives for many states to forgo more rigorous standards in favor of ones that districts were more likely to meet. It's not that we have too few standards, but rather that we have too many. And too many of them are too low, contributing to unequal access to educational opportunities for students on the basis of where they live, and to the low performance of U.S. students in international comparisons.

This must be remedied. When standards in Mississippi and Tennessee are dramatically lower than those in New York, Massachusetts, and California, long-standing inequities get perpetuated every September with each new class of kindergartners. With U.S. fifteen-year-olds ranked twenty-fifth among thirty industrialized nations on the Organization for Economic Cooperation and Development's (OECD) international mathematics exam and twenty-fourth in science, the time has come for leaders across the political and philosophical spectrum to put aside ideology in favor of the next generation's ability to compete globally.

As *Leading for Equity* went to press, President Obama and his secretary of education Arne Duncan had begun talking with the states' governors about the possibility of creating a set of rigorous *voluntary* national standards. These standards should focus on rigorous content knowledge in reading, math, and science, as well as on students' abilities to apply that knowledge through demonstrations of critical thinking and problem solving. One viable option is to adapt the OECD international benchmarks for fifteen-year-old students to the U.S. context and backward map them to the early grades, using the value chain approach we saw in Montgomery County.

In order for voluntary standards to take hold, states must have meaningful incentives to embrace them. One way to do this is to make adoption a prerequisite for accessing investment capital from Secretary Duncan's $5 billion Race to the Top fund. States and districts could apply for funds to help them create the capacity they need to ensure that teachers and school leaders have the knowledge, skills, and tools necessary to diagnose student learning needs and differentiate their response so that every child has the opportunity to meet the high standards. The federal Department of Education (DOE) could create another incentive for national standards by paying for the development and scoring of common assessments, thereby freeing up the significant dollars currently tied up in the overhead required to maintain fifty different standards and testing regimes. These state resources could be reallocated away from administrative costs toward innovations in effective ways to help students meet rigorous standards, leading to a cycle of improvement nationally that would outpace anything that has come before. And though it would be controversial, if some states insist on clinging to mediocre standards that consign vast numbers of their children to low-wage work, the DOE should eventually consider ways to significantly reduce their flow of federal education dollars if evidence shows positive effects in states that have implemented the national standards.

The creation and adoption of voluntary national standards is a dramatic shift from the status quo. It could be an important piece of the puzzle that we need to solve in order to significantly raise the sights of our next generation. In his first speech to Congress on February 24, 2009, President Obama set a new goal of having the highest proportion of college graduates in the world by 2020, and called on young people to stay in school, saying that dropping out is "not just quitting on yourself, it's quitting on your country."[5] In his 2009 annual letter about the work of his foundation, Bill Gates proposed a national goal of having 80 percent of high school students graduate ready for college by 2025.[6] We are a long way from these goals, but they are attainable. Setting a few clear, high standards for what it means in the United States to graduate from high school ready for college is an important step, as is the adoption of a set of common benchmarks aligned with those standards from the early grades up through high school. This is the path Montgomery County chose, and it is on the way to having 80 percent of its students graduating ready for college by 2014.

Eight years ago, no one thought that building agreement for national standards was possible, which is why they were not a part of the NCLB compromise. Is it possible now? Perhaps, but only if parents, students, community activists, superintendents, teachers, union leaders, education entrepreneurs, business leaders, and policy makers demand that we have them. Pressure from many quarters could build into a movement for change that would be impossible to ignore and could force the country's political leaders to break away from the old arguments that for too long have distracted us from keeping our national promise of public education as the "great equalizer" for access to unlimited opportunities. What will it take? As in Montgomery County, it will take a broad-based coalition willing to lead for equity.

CHAPTER EIGHT

Strategy as Problem Solving— Applying the MCPS Approach

Many school districts (and businesses, for that matter) are great at articulating a vision and developing compelling mission statements and bulky strategic plans, but what sets the MCPS team apart ... is that it actually implements—it does what it plans to do.

In some ways, the journey that MCPS has been on since 1999 has been a series of increasingly sophisticated problem-solving exercises. In the early days, Weast and his team had a general sense of the inequities between subgroups of students, which were being exacerbated by the way the district did business. The data showed geographic differences in performance in a number of content areas, and this led to the Red Zone/Green Zone strategy. As the team dug deeper, it developed richer insights about the root causes of the performance differences. These included inconsistencies in the expectations for students as they moved from kindergarten through twelfth grade or transferred from one school to another, the lack of capacity of many school teams to serve students with different learning needs, and individual beliefs about the level at which certain kinds of children could achieve.[1]

Along the way, Weast and his team developed theories of action for addressing these and the many other root causes that they uncovered as they put plans into action. While the implementation of the initial theory was complex, the idea itself was simple. If teachers believe that every child can master high-level content, and they have the training, tools, and support they need to identify gaps in student learning and differentiate their instruction to meet these needs, then they will be effective with all of their students, and the link between race, class, and achievement will be broken.

This theory led to an evolving academic strategy with a set of coherent actions, including defining the Pathway to Success, instituting all-day kindergarten, backward mapping the mathematics curriculum, focusing on literacy in the early grades, developing formative assessments at every level, setting a target that all students complete algebra by the end of eighth grade, and designing a whole set of high school interventions that centered on access to honors and AP courses. Over time, the district adapted the strategy as it made progress on some performance problems and not others. And as we described in chapters 4, 5, and 6, the team was relentless about creating an organizational context that supported and held accountable teachers, principals, and central office staff as they went about the hard work of implementing the strategy.

In this final chapter, we describe a problem-solving process developed by faculty members of the Public Education Leadership Project (PELP) at Harvard University. The process facilitates the design and implementation of a strategy for continuous improvement and is one way to summarize important parts of the MCPS story.[2] In addition to explaining the process, we provide key questions that leadership teams should ask themselves at each step in the process, as well as brief illustrative examples from MCPS.

OVERVIEW

The problem-solving approach to designing and implementing a strategy includes seven steps, pictured in figure 8.1:

1. Identify and analyze the problem.

2. Develop a theory of action.

3. Design the strategy.

4. Plan for implementation.

5. Implement the strategy.

6. Assess progress.

7. Adapt and modify for continuous improvement.

Teams rarely move through each step sequentially, and might get stuck and revisit earlier steps throughout the process. For instance, when MCPS decided to replace teacher recommendations with PSAT scores as the criteria for acceptance into AP classes, it could move only so far around the problem-solving loop before having to backtrack to an earlier step. MCPS knew that PSAT scores were a good predictor of

FIG. 8.1 **A problem-solving approach to strategy design and implementation**

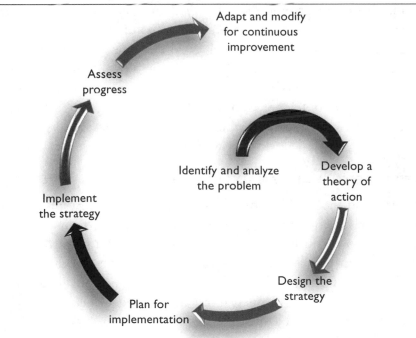

success in AP courses and decided to use PSAT participation to open up broader access to AP courses, a key piece of its academic strategy. But black and Hispanic students were opting out of the PSAT at disproportionate rates, and even though the district decreed that schools boost PSAT participation to 100 percent, test taking among minority students did not accelerate nearly as fast as the district hoped.

Under the leadership of deputy superintendent Frieda Lacey, members of the leadership team went back to the drawing board and then conducted field visits and interviews with students and teachers. What they heard helped them realize that the underlying belief system that students had about themselves and the expectations some teachers had of certain types of students created a barrier the team members had not foreseen in their implementation planning. They created the honors/AP identification tool, HAPIT, and revised the implementation plan to include PSAT participation rates on principal and school evaluations, so that the accountability system became aligned with the strategy. They also developed a communication plan to help students and their families better understand the value of taking the test. PSAT participation rates began to improve dramatically, followed by black and Hispanic AP enrollment. This is a good example of moving to the implementation stage, and then later revisiting the problem identification stage when results do not match initial expectations. Through constant review and adaptation, MCPS has been able to realize continuous improvement on a number of academic indicators.

STEP 1: IDENTIFY AND ANALYZE THE PROBLEM

The first and most critical step in solving a performance problem is to accurately identify and rigorously analyze it. If a team does not take this step seriously, a lack of rigor can result in a weak theory of action. At first glance, this may seem to be the easiest of the steps in the process—after all, it is not difficult to brainstorm a long list of problems. However, it is much more challenging to figure out what is really going on. Problem definitions that focus on blaming others, such as "There isn't enough money," or "The union is against it," or

"If only parents would . . . ," are tempting because they can absolve schools and districts of the responsibility for taking action. MCPS was willing to identify its own practices at the school and central office level that were contributing to student performance problems. As author Rick DuFour puts it, rather than focusing outward on forces over which it had little control, MCPS focused on problems that were within its sphere of influence. DuFour calls this looking "in the mirror" instead of "out the window."[3] As the district made progress on key indicators, its sphere of influence expanded, making it possible to address some factors later in its journey that it never could have taken on when it was starting out.

MCPS tackled a number of performance problems by focusing on the critical work that happens in classrooms, sometimes referred to as the *instructional core* of schools. The instructional core is the interaction of three components: the skill and knowledge of *teachers*, the engagement of *students* in their own learning, and rigorous academic content.[4] In MCPS's problem analysis, other important issues (resources, stakeholders, politics, etc.) emerged as contributing factors to the achievement gap or as implementation challenges, but the team did not use those issues as excuses for ignoring the hard work of making classrooms stronger.

In defining and addressing problems, it is important to engage a range of participants who can contribute firsthand knowledge and insight based on their recent experience in classrooms and schools, as well as their knowledge of the broader community. As we described in chapter 1, when Weast and his team held town hall–style meetings all over the county in the first few months of his tenure, they were not simply selling a plan—they were engaging the community in a problem identification process that led to *Our Call to Action*. The process not only led to widespread ownership of the manifesto; it also made the content much stronger because it included multiple perspectives about the nature of the problems facing the district. Below are some questions leadership teams can use to begin identifying and analyzing a performance problem. After the list of questions, we will describe one method of uncovering root causes, a key activity in this step of the process.

- What is the performance problem we are trying to solve? Describe it in simple terms with no jargon (no more than a sentence or two). Be sure that it is linked to activities and outcomes related to the instructional core (students, teachers, academic content).

- What concrete evidence do we have to back up the short description we developed? Will this evidence enable us to communicate the nature and importance of the problem to staff and stakeholders? How will we test our assumptions with them and learn from their feedback?

- What are three or four observable symptoms of the problem we identified? (Your team should have a wide-ranging brainstorming session to come up with as many symptoms as you can name, and then refine the list into categories to make the process more manageable.)

- What are the root causes of each symptom? (More on root cause analysis below.)

- Is it possible to prioritize the root causes that emerge from our analysis? Often, it is not possible to do everything at once, and your team should develop a common point of view about where to start. One way to force your team to prioritize is by asking, "If we had time or money to tackle only one or two root causes, which ones do we believe would have the most impact?"

- What are the consequences of *not* solving the problem? Be specific. How will a failure to act affect students over the long term? How will it impact districtwide performance in the medium term?

Table 8.1 provides an example of a root cause analysis technique called the "five whys." The method is widely used in various continuous improvement processes.[5] Once a team has identified a performance problem and its symptoms, it tries to uncover root causes by asking "Why?" in a systematic manner, over and over, until it reaches

TABLE 8.1 **Root cause analysis guide (with example)**

Problem: In our district, there are significant differences in academic outcomes between subgroups of students K–12, predictable largely by the race and ethnicity of the students.

Symptom 1: By grade 3, gaps are present on state reading exams. African American and Hispanic students, on average, score 20 points lower than white and Asian students.	Symptom 2: Our high school AP and honors courses are disproportionally enrolled in by white and Asian students.
Why? We have anecdotal evidence that students come to kindergarten with different levels of pre-literacy skills, but no hard data about the nature and scale of the differences for individual students, or how they progress.	**Why?** African American and Hispanic students enroll in AP and honors courses at much lower rates than their overall percentage of the student body.
Why? We don't perform diagnostic assessments of students in grades K–2.	**Why?** Fewer students in these subgroups have the prerequisites, especially in mathematics.
Why? We don't have valid tools to diagnose or respond to the different learning needs of students in these early grades.	**Why?** Very low numbers of African American and Hispanic students have completed algebra by grade 8.
Why? We have not invested in the tools our teachers need for diagnosis or the skills or curriculum they need to effectively differentiate.	**Why?** When we begin sorting students into different math ability levels in fourth grade, these students are disproportionately assigned to the "regular" math track.
~~Why?~~	**Why?** Many students are not getting what they need for success in K–3 math, and the others are often placed in courses below their ability levels.

an actionable root cause. Experts say this usually takes five *whys*, hence the name of the method.

The table describes a performance problem that MCPS shares with many urban districts and two common, observable symptoms of that problem that were present in Montgomery County when the district began its journey. Each column has a series of questions—*whys*—for each symptom, moving down the columns of the table. Arranging the example in a table might signal that the process is linear, but root cause analysis is not an exact science. Groups working together to identify symptoms and causes usually engage in free-form brainstorming for a significant amount of time before being ready to drill down on any one issue.

Sometimes a team might only need to go through four *whys* to uncover a root cause, as in symptom 1 in the table, and sometimes it might take six. The number is not as important as working together to find an actionable root cause. Most problems have more than two symptoms, and symptoms can have more than one root cause. In order to keep the illustration as simple as possible, we chose only two symptoms and show the root cause process once for each. Clearly, additional or alternative paths exist for each symptom, and it is important for teams to explore multiple options in their analysis.

Here is how a conversation might sound using the five *whys* for symptom 1, "By third grade, gaps are present on state reading exams":

Question 1: *Why* are gaps evident on state reading exams by third grade?

Answer: Because African American and Hispanic students, on average, score 20 points lower than white and Asian students.

Question 2: *Why* do African American and Hispanic students, on average, score 20 points lower than white and Asian students?

Answer: We are not sure. We have anecdotal evidence that students come to kindergarten with different levels of pre-literacy skills, but no hard data about the nature and scale of the differences for individual students, or how they progress.

Question 3: *Why* don't we have hard data about the nature and scale of the differences for individual students, or how they progress?

Answer: We don't perform diagnostic assessments of students in grades K–2.

Question 4: *Why* don't we perform diagnostic assessments of students in grades K through 2?

Answer: We don't have valid tools to diagnose or respond to the different learning needs of students in these early grades.

Question 5: *Why* don't we have valid tools to diagnose or respond to the different learning needs of students in these early grades?

Answer: We have not invested in the tools our teachers need for diagnosis or the skills or curriculum they need to effectively differentiate.

In this example, the root cause analysis takes a twist at question 3, because MCPS realized it did not have a system in place to provide the data it needed to answer question 2. The remaining questions address this lack of knowledge. The bottom line was that the district simply was not investing in the kinds of tools and technology that teachers needed to address early literacy problems. In chapter 5, we discussed the diagnostic assessments on wireless handheld devices that MCPS developed in partnership with Wireless Generation in response to this root cause.

STEP 2: DEVELOP A THEORY OF ACTION

The next step in the problem-solving process is to articulate a theory of action for how to address the problem by attacking its root causes. As with any theory, a district's theory of action is a statement about cause and effect. In other words, which actions does the team think will lead to its desired results? The elements of the theory of action should map back to the root causes uncovered in the earlier problem analysis. Using "if . . . then . . ." statements to articulate the theory of action can help ensure that the theory stays focused on testable predictions about cause and effect rather than ideology or personal philosophy. At the beginning of this chapter, we described an early version of MCPS's theory of action; this became much more sophisticated as it learned over time and went deeper into the implementation of its differentiation strategy. It starts with a statement of assumptions and then describes the theory of action that drove much of the work described in earlier chapters:

> All students should have access to rigorous academic content, which they can master if they are adequately prepared beginning in kindergarten. We believe that our teachers are committed to their students' learning, but might not have the skills or curriculum they need. We acknowledge that our entire system currently has institutional barriers that (a) sort children away from our most rigorous courses and (b) thereby reinforce widely held but inaccurate assumptions about the ability of all children to master rigorous content if given the right supports. Therefore, if we:
>
> 1. Invest heavily in diagnostic assessment, differentiated instruction, and effective literacy curriculum beginning in kindergarten
>
> 2. Remove the institutional barriers and sorting mechanisms that begin as early as fourth grade
>
> 3. Open up access to rigorous high school courses rather than viewing them as appropriate for only a few
>
> 4. Give our principals and teachers all of the support they need to change their practice and their beliefs in order to meet the new expectations . . .
>
> Then, over time, not only will we eliminate achievement gaps that are predictable by race and ethnicity; we will also raise the bar for all of our students because of our focus on rigorous coursework for every child.

Below is a set of questions teams can ask themselves to develop a theory of action.

- What specific actions do we think will reduce or eliminate the effects of one or more of the root causes we identified in the previous step? Answer this question for as many root causes as you can.

- Why do we think these actions will lead to the results we desire? In other words, what assumptions are we making about how kids learn? How adults learn? How our team operates? About our context or environment? About our students and their families? Another way to think about this step is, What do we have to believe for our theory to have merit? As you will notice in the example above, stating these assumptions up front can help everyone understand what beliefs underpin your theory of action.

- From the above analysis, construct a series of "if . . . then . . ." statements that communicate the theory of action.

STEP 3: DESIGN THE STRATEGY

A strategy is simply the set of coherent actions a district takes to put its theory into practice and address the problems it has identified. It should include the target of the intervention (particular student groups, grade levels, content areas, or employee groups), the specific actions that will be taken, and the timetable for implementation and results. In addition to identifying the activities of the strategy in this step, leadership teams should diagnose the degree to which the organization's structures, systems, resources, culture, and stakeholder relationships are coherent with the strategy.

Below is an example of a four-part strategy statement that describes much of MCPS's work described in this book. Note that it includes concrete actions, the groups affected, benchmarks, and timelines. It is also consistent with the previously described theory of action.

- We will deploy a new K–2 diagnostic literacy assessment for every child, along with the technology, curriculum, and training for our teachers to use the assessments and make differentiated instructional decisions based on the results. We will begin the rollout next fall and be fully operational in eighteen months. Every kindergartner entering our system in fall 2010 will be assessed and taught with this new approach. By the third year of full implementation, we expect 80 percent of our kindergartners to finish the year with 90 percent or above proficiency in preliteracy skills, with no significant differences by race or ethnicity. We expect that using this approach, K–2 will translate into similar results on the third-grade state reading exam.

- We will immediately allow high school students to sign up for advanced placement and honors courses without the requirement of a teacher's recommendation. We realize that students need an academic foundation to be successful in these courses, so we will still have requirements, such as scoring at certain levels on the PSAT in relevant subjects. All students will be required to take the PSAT, and principals will be held accountable for participation rates so that taking the test does not become another barrier. If these changes result in oversubscription of higher-level courses, we will invest in expanding capacity to meet the demand. Over several years, we expect the changes we are making in the early grades to dramatically increase demand for AP and honors courses, and will begin to prepare now for that projected demand.

- We will backward map the AP content standards for advanced math courses such as calculus and statistics all the way to kindergarten and align our curriculum with these standards so that every child in our system has an equal opportunity to master rigorous high school math content. As a result, we expect 90 percent of our students to complete algebra by the eighth grade starting five years into implementation. We will begin to prepare now for increased demand for sixth-, seventh-, and eighth-grade algebra classes as we make staffing decisions and provide professional development.

- Every teacher, principal, and central office administrator will be held accountable for goals that are in line with this strategy and relevant to their own roles. Because this new approach requires a dramatic shift in the expectations of teachers, principals, staff, students, and parents, we will begin aligning all of our organizational systems and structures, resources, and culture to help people change their practices and beliefs to support the new strategy.

This is a comprehensive academic strategy. Introducing a new academic strategy usually requires a number of supporting systems and structures, as we have seen in the MCPS story, especially in chapters 4 and 5. Creating the professional growth system, strengthening peer assistance and review, providing a source for student achievement data to support quick decision making, implementing M-STAT, conducting diversity training, and launching the Professional Learning Communities Institute are all examples of new or adapted systems and structures that were critically important to the effectiveness of the academic strategy. The problem-solving approach discussed in this chapter is also relevant and valuable for designing and implementing plans to create or change organizational systems and structures that support a strategy.

The following questions can be helpful in developing a concrete strategy:

- What set of actions will we take to put our theory of action into practice? How do the specific actions map back to the assumptions about cause and effect that underpin our theory of action?

- Who will be affected by our actions (students, stakeholders, employees)?

- What is a reasonable time frame over which the actions have to be consistently implemented to achieve results? (Build this directly into your strategy statement.)

- Are the relevant systems, structures, resources, and culture of our organization likely to make it easier or harder to effectively implement the strategy? If they make it harder, what changes are needed in order to increase the likelihood that we can implement the strategy well?[6] What are the specific short-, medium-, and long-term targets we will hit if our strategy is successful?

STEP 4: PLAN FOR IMPLEMENTATION

Preparing to implement the strategy is as important as implementation. In this step, teams should identify the resources needed to successfully execute the strategy. These might include financial resources, people, and/or technology. A team should pay particular attention to the people aspects of the implementation plan. A strategy's success or failure is largely dependent on the ability of the relevant staff members to perform the tasks that make the strategy come to life, and it is important to identify knowledge or skill gaps in the planning phase. The same is true of political support, both within the system and outside it.

MCPS engaged in the Baldrige quality process, which includes a rigorous implementation-planning format. For every big initiative, from full-day kindergarten and early-grade literacy to the implementation of M-STAT and the new grading and reporting system, stakeholders around the system were involved not only in the design of the initiative, but also in the planning for implementation.

However, on a couple of occasions, district employees agreed that the rush to implement might have hampered the early effectiveness of new projects. For instance, when the Wireless Generation product was launched, the initial plan called for a 19-school pilot for several months, with full rollout to all 129 elementary schools over two years. As described in chapter 5, because Weast was so excited about the results from the early stages of the pilot, he pushed the district's CIO and company executives to accelerate the rollout in order to have every school up and running within five months.

The technology was ready, but several unexpected factors related to the user experience emerged during the rollout, and the entire project had to be suspended while the technology team sorted out the issues. In the meantime, teachers wondered whether this new gadget was really going to be worth all of the trouble. After a review of the implementation plan that included classroom observations of nonpilot school teachers using the device, a new rollout schedule was developed. After productive discussions with teachers union president Bonnie Cullison, the district hired substitutes to cover teachers' classrooms while they used the product for the first time with individual students. This allowed teachers to take sufficient time to learn the technology and use it at a comfortable pace with their students in the early days. The story has a happy ending: three years later, teachers would fight to keep the tool if someone threatened to take it away. But had the development of the original implementation plan included the voice of classroom teachers in schools not participating in the pilot, the early problems might have been avoided.[7]

Questions to ask during this step are as follows:

- What steps will we take to implement our strategy? *Who* will do *what* by *when*?

- What material resources are required to implement the strategy? (Curricular materials, technology, physical space, etc.)

- Is new training needed to ensure that the people asked to implement pieces of the strategy have the skills they need to do their best work?

- How much will the implementation cost? How will we pay for it? Will there be savings in other areas related to the new strategy?

- What are the implications for teachers, principals, and central office staff if nothing changes? This question helps uncover particular groups that might feel threatened by the changes you propose.

- How will we build support for the strategy, especially among stakeholder groups who think that they may lose out as a result of the change?

- What roadblocks (both internal and external) are we likely to encounter? What can we do to prevent or quickly address them? Who will be accountable for managing the response to roadblocks?

- Who (individual or group) will "own" the implementation—in other words, who will ensure that people and schools have what they need and are actually performing the work necessary for a successful implementation?

- What are some specific benchmarks we will measure throughout the process to assess whether or not the implementation is on track? What indicators will let us know whether the strategy is as effective as we imagine it will be? What measures should we put in place to assess the validity of our theory of action and test the assumptions embedded in the theory?

- Are there systems in place to collect the data needed for the indicators developed above? If not how will we create them? Who will be responsible for analyzing the data that is gathered? Is there an existing team that is the logical group to make decisions based on the analysis? If not, should we create an ad hoc team for this purpose? Who should be part of this team?

STEP 5: IMPLEMENT THE STRATEGY

During this step, people must have the resources, knowledge, skills, and support they need at all times in order to implement the strategy with fidelity. While this sounds straightforward, the implementation phase is where great strategies go to die—in business as well as in education. To paraphrase a business cliché, a second-rate strategy that is well implemented always beats a first-rate strategy that is poorly implemented.

During implementation, district leaders need to take the time to ensure that everyone understands the strategy, how his or her particular job or task contributes to the overall effort, and why it is important. District leaders must also solicit feedback and suggestions from those who are implementing the strategy—typically teachers and principals.

In addition to the necessary skills, employees must have the will to implement. Often, school districts adopt a "volunteer" approach to implementation. If people engage in the new strategy, that's great. If they do not, leaders bemoan the lack of fidelity of implementation, but often take little or no action to understand why things are not working or to change staff behavior. Accountability mechanisms are necessary to reinforce the new behaviors being asked of people and to ensure that school and central office staff are engaged in those behaviors. They can also be important in uncovering parts of the implementation plan in need of adjustment. But mechanisms are not enough—leaders must have the managerial courage to enforce consequences when staff members choose not to engage in the strategy.

Chapters 1 through 6 of this book demonstrate clearly that educators in Montgomery County are focused on implementation. Many school districts (and businesses, for that matter) are great at articulating a vision and developing compelling mission statements and bulky strategic plans, but what sets the MCPS team apart from many of these organizations is that it actually implements—it does what it plans to do. Though at times it took patience and hard work to bring the staff along, implementation of the district strategy was expected, and over the long term "volunteerism" was not a viable option.

When Weast and his team developed the Red Zone strategy and the focus on early-grade literacy, as well as the access/rigor/equity framework, they did more than simply announce it and expect that everyone would automatically follow along. Investing in innovative professional development, such as the Professional Learning Communities Institute, was critical to giving teachers and principals the skills and tools they needed to implement successfully. Engaging in a constant give-and-take with union leadership over the interests and needs of teachers around the district helped the rollout plans become more robust and the implementation of key initiatives happen more effectively. Communicating with employees and community stakeholders constantly was more than simply a public relations ploy—it helped smooth the way for more difficult aspects of the strategy as it evolved.

For any district team implementing a strategy, roadblocks will surely arise, and they must be addressed immediately. Usually, these barriers can be overcome, but occasionally a bump in the road is an opportunity to learn important information that will help improve the strategy. Feedback loops that enable the organization to learn and continuously improve are critical to successful implementation over time. Guiding questions for the implementation step include the following:

- Do people understand how their day-to-day actions are related to the strategy? Is the strategy meaningful to them?

- Are we providing the supports people need to enable them to successfully perform the work required of them during the implementation phase?

- Are people actually implementing the strategy as it was designed? If not, why not? Are there consequences for failing to implement the strategy?

- What is the process for making sure that all participants provide regular feedback that will allow us to continuously improve performance by adapting the strategy as we learn?

STEP 6: ASSESS PROGRESS

While implementation is under way, leaders should be collecting, analyzing, and making decisions based on data about three dimensions: (1) the progress of the implementation, (2) the effectiveness of the strategy, and (3) the validity of the theory of action.

In Montgomery County, district leaders implemented the M-STAT process that we described in chapters 5 and 6. M-STAT created a concrete mechanism through which school teams could talk with each other and with central office staff on a regular basis about aspects of the strategy and its implementation, with an eye toward assessing progress and planning for improvement.

During M-STAT meetings, school leaders review their progress on key goals, discussed areas of success, and reflected on areas for improvement. Each of these activities is useful for assessing the effectiveness of the implementation, the strength of the strategy, and the soundness of the underlying theory of action. The process helps uncover roadblocks and resource constraints that need attention so that school teams can be more effective. It also highlights knowledge and skill gaps among school staffs that the district can help address more effectively at scale.

As district teams think about assessing the progress of a strategy and its implementation, the following questions can be useful guides:

Implementation

- Are the data we are gathering the best data for assessing our progress? Are we asking the relevant stakeholders to give us input about the implementation?

- Are we achieving all of the milestones we set during the implementation-planning step? Are we on track in terms of timelines? Budget projections? Staff allocations?

- If we are missing milestones, why is that happening? Was the initial schedule unrealistically ambitious? Did we underestimate the time certain activities would take to accomplish? Did our forecasts fail to account for important factors? Have barriers come up that were unexpected? Should we adjust our expectations or accelerate our efforts in order to meet our original targets?

- Are individuals and/or teams engaging productively in the activities that the strategy requires? If not, why? Is it a problem of skill, which would call for us to provide more training and development? Or is it a problem of will? Are some people opting out of the whole approach, believing that "this too shall pass"? If so, what steps will we take to help people change their behavior? If this is ineffective, what will we do?

- If our implementation seems on track but we are missing our targets, should we reexamine our strategy or our theory of action? Did we misdiagnose the root causes of the problem?

Strategy

- Assuming that our implementation indicators are positive, do the interim performance results in the areas in which our strategy should have impact match the expectations we had during the design phase?

- If not, what can we learn from our feedback loops that might help us revise the strategy to make it more effective? Are there alternative activities that might be more powerful?

Theory of Action

- What do our interim results tell us about our predictions about cause and effect?

- Have we learned anything during implementation of our strategy that challenges any of the assumptions embedded in our theory? About our diagnosis of root causes?

STEP 7: ADAPT AND MODIFY FOR CONTINUOUS IMPROVEMENT

Throughout the implementation of the strategy, a team might discover new problems or miss original targets. By adapting and modifying the implementation plan, the strategy, and the theory of action as more information becomes available, districts can accelerate their progress. Modifications could be as simple as addressing an unforeseen skill gap in key personnel or as complicated as adapting to changes in state regulations. Alternatively, changes might mean clarifying the original intent of the strategy so that people in the organization engage in activities that are aimed at the true purpose rather than easier but less effective actions.

For instance, when MCPS began to focus on minority AP enrollments in its drive for access and rigor, the aggregate numbers looked good—minority student enrollment in AP courses did rise after the PSAT participation rates went up. But the M-STAT process enabled district and school leaders to systematically examine the story behind the numbers. What they found was that most of the enrollment increases were coming from "soft" courses like psychology. While this was in some ways good news, it was not the full intent of the strategy, which was to ensure that minority students were enrolling in higher-level math and science courses like calculus and physics so that they would be better prepared for competitive colleges. Weast and his team responded by adapting the strategy to include more concrete enrollment targets for AP math and science courses, but they did not stop there. By listening to staff and students about the obstacles that kept enrollment low in these courses, the district developed additional supports for students and their teachers to be successful in more challenging math and science classes. This included professional development for teachers and intensive academic support for students, but it also pushed the district to think more granularly about the path from kindergarten to high school. This eventually was manifested in the goal to have 80 percent of all students complete algebra before entering ninth grade—a clear gateway to AP content in high school.

As teams pursue the difficult work of solving performance problems, they should take time to recognize when they make real progress in tackling the root causes that contribute to the problems. Every September at Weast's back-to-school talks, he recognized schools for their progress on key indicators while also continuing to make the case for the strategy and its acceleration. Every year the *Our Call to Action* annual report highlighted great progress while pointing toward new performance horizons to reach together.

Questions that can help teams in thinking about this ongoing step are the following:

- How should we respond to the information generated in the "assess" step?

- If we are making progress in solving the initial problem we identified, what adjustments do we need to make to our approach now that one or more of the root causes might be diminishing in importance?

- How can we create opportunities for the people involved in the work to celebrate progress while maintaining a sense of urgency about solving difficult performance problems over the long term?

CONCLUSION

Adopting a problem-solving approach to strategy and implementation is an effective way for teams to produce better outcomes for students across a school district by thinking through the development of a strategy and implementing it with both discipline and flexibility over time. MCPS internalized the approach as a way of analyzing and addressing problems, but isn't in love with the process for its own sake. For the district, it is a habit of mind that has become a way of doing business, not a formal exercise.

Because the process is focused on continuous improvement, the goal isn't to get the problem analysis or strategy formulation "right" the first time, but to have a clear-eyed view of the challenges and an orientation toward getting better and better over time. This way of operating can effectively focus the attention and efforts of multiple stakeholder groups on identifying and tackling tough problems. Continuous improvement is by its nature a never-ending journey, but one that can be rewarding when educators and stakeholders who are committed to their students see the results of a deliberate and strategic approach to solving performance problems.

Notes

Introduction

1. John Dewey, *The School and Society* (Chicago: University of Chicago Press, 1902), 3.
2. Karen L. Mapp, David A. Thomas, and Tonika Cheek Clayton, "Race, Accountability, and the Achievement Gap (B)," Case PEL-044 (Boston: Harvard Business School, 2006), 2–3.

Chapter 1

1. Edmund Gordon, *The Gordon Report: A Study of Minority Achievement in MCPS—If Not Now, When; If Not Here, Where?* (Pomona, NY: Gordon and Gordon Associates, 1990), 374.
2. Jerry Weast, interview by author, from a series of interviews with him conducted in person in Rockville, MD, or by telephone, October 2008–January 2009.
3. Montgomery County Public Schools, *Our Call to Action: Raising the Bar and Closing the Gap* (Rockville, MD: Montgomery County Public Schools, 1999).
4. Ibid.
5. Ibid.
6. Ibid.
7. Richard Elmore, David A. Thomas, and Tonika Cheek Clayton, "Differentiated Treatment in Montgomery County Public Schools," Case 9-PEL-028 (Boston: Harvard Business School, 2006), 6.
8. Ibid.
9. Scott Thompson, "Breaking the Links Between Race, Poverty, and Achievement," *Strategies for School System Leaders on District-Level Change* 13, no.1 (2007): 8.
10. Ibid.

Chapter 2

1. Richard Elmore, David A. Thomas, and Tonika Cheek Clayton, "Differentiated Treatment in Montgomery County Public Schools," Case 9-PEL-028 (Boston: Harvard Business School, 2006), 3.
2. Ibid., 4.
3. Karen L. Mapp, David A. Thomas, and Tonika Cheek Clayton, "Race, Accountability, and the Achievement Gap (A)," Case 9-PEL-043 (Boston: Harvard Business School, 2006), 5.
4. Dale Fulton, written communication to author, October 23, 2008.

5. Mapp, Thomas, and Clayton, "Race, Accountability, and the Achievement Gap (A)," 5.
6. Elmore, Thomas, and Clayton, "Differentiated Treatment in Montgomery County Public Schools," 7.
7. Jerry Weast, interview by author, from a series of interviews with him conducted in person in Rockville, MD, or by telephone, October 2008–January 2009.

Chapter 3

1. Roger Fisher and William Ury, *Getting to Yes: Negotiating Agreement Without Giving In*, 2nd ed. (New York: Penguin Books, 1991).
2. Bonnie Cullison, e-mail message to author, November 19, 2008.
3. Jerry Weast, interview by author. All interviews with Weast quoted from in this chapter were conducted in person in Rockville, MD, or by telephone, October 2008–January 2009.
4. Patricia O'Neill, written communication to author, November 9, 2008.
5. Weast interview.
6. Montgomery County Business Roundtable for Education (MCBRE), "MCBRE Sends MCPS Emerging Student Leaders to the Congressional Black Caucus and Congressional Hispanic Caucus Annual Public Policy Conferences," *The Bridge*, January 2007, 2.
7. Montgomery County Public Schools, Ruth Rales Comcast Kids Reading Network, "About the Reading Network," http://www.montgomeryschoolsmd.org/readingnetwork/docs/RuthRalesFlyer.pdf.

Chapter 4

1. Montgomery County Public Schools, *Our Call to Action: Raising the Bar and Closing the Gap* (Rockville, MD: Montgomery County Public Schools, 1999).
2. Jerry Weast, telephone conversation with author, March 18, 2009.
3. MCPS Professional Learning Institute, "Rising to the Challenge: The Case of Broad Acres Elementary" (case study, July 2005), 15.
4. Jerry Weast, interview by author, from a series of interviews with him conducted in person in Rockville, MD, or by telephone, October 2008–January 2009.
5. Jamie Virga and Joan Mory, "The Professional Learning Communities Institute: Building PLCs in MCPS," *Journal of Staff Development* (Summer 2008).
6. Karen L. Mapp, David A. Thomas, and Tonika Cheek Clayton, "Race, Accountability, and the Achievement Gap (A)," Case 9-PEL-043 (Boston: Harvard Business School, 2006), 13.

Chapter 5

1. Richard Elmore, David A. Thomas, and Tonika Cheek Clayton, "Differentiated Treatment in Montgomery County Public Schools," Case 9-PEL-028 (Boston: Harvard Business School, 2006), 9.

2. Stacey Childress, "Wireless Generation," Case 9-307-049 (Boston: Harvard Business School, 2008), 6.
3. Ibid., 9.
4. Ibid., 9–10.
5. Jerry Weast, interview by author. All interviews with Weast quoted from in this chapter were conducted in person in Rockville, MD, or by telephone, October 2008–March 2009.
6. *Strategies for School System Leaders on District-Level Change* 13, no. 1 (2007): 8.
7. Weast interview.
8. Jody Leleck, e-mail message to author, November 18, 2008.
9. Karen L. Mapp, David A. Thomas, and Tonika Cheek Clayton, "Race, Accountability, and the Achievement Gap (B)," Case PEL-044 (Boston: Harvard Business School, 2006), 4.
10. Anonymous superintendent's e-mail message to author, November 11, 2008.
11. Ibid., 6.
12. Ibid.
13. Donna Hollingshead, e-mail message to author, November 11, 2008.

Chapter 6

1. This chapter draws heavily on two cases written by Karen Mapp, David Thomas, and Tonika Cheek Clayton of the Public Education Leadership Project at Harvard University. All quotes in the chapter are excerpted from these pieces unless otherwise noted. The authors thank Mapp and Cheek Clayton for their invaluable contributions to this chapter.
2. Richard Elmore, David A. Thomas, and Tonika Cheek Clayton, "Differentiated Treatment in Montgomery County Public Schools," Case 9-PEL-028 (Boston: Harvard Business School, 2006), 10.
3. Brian J. Porter, Daniel Curry-Corcoran, and Kecia Addison-Scott, *Moving Beyond Stereotypes: The Case of Viers Mill Elementary* (Rockville, MD: Montgomery County Public Schools, Professional Learning Communities Institute, 2005), 13.
4. Ibid., 14.
5. Karen L. Mapp, David A. Thomas, and Tonika Cheek Clayton, "Race, Accountability, and the Achievement Gap (B)," Case PEL-044 (Boston: Harvard Business School, 2006), 2–3.
6. Ibid., 3.
7. Julie Wade, *Evaluation of Montgomery County Public Schools Study Circle Program* (Rockville, MD: Montgomery County Public Schools, Department of Shared Accountability, 2007), 10.
8. Ibid., 13.
9. Jerry Weast, telephone conversation with author, November 18, 2008.
10. Donna Graves, interview by author, Rockville, MD, October 29, 2008.
11. Ibid.

Chapter 7

1. Thomas L. Friedman, "Obama's Real Test," *New York Times*, March 17, 2009.
2. Jerry Weast, telephone conversation with author, March 18, 2009.
3. Jerry Weast, telephone conversation with author, November 7, 2008.
4. Karen L. Mapp, David A. Thomas, and Tonika Cheek Clayton, "Race, Accountability, and the Achievement Gap (B)," Case PEL-044 (Boston: Harvard Business School, 2006), 3.
5. President Barack Obama, address to joint session of Congress, February 24, 2009.
6. "2009 Annual Letter from Bill Gates: U.S. Education," Bill & Melinda Gates Foundation, http://www.gatesfoundation.org/annual-letter/Pages/2009-united-states-education.aspx.

Chapter 8

1. This chapter draws heavily on Stacey Childress and Geoff Marietta, "A Problem-Solving Approach to Designing and Implementing a Strategy to Improve Performance," Case 9-PEL-056 (Boston: Harvard Business School, 2008). Stacey Childress would like to thank her PELP colleagues for their contributions to the original publication as well as for their support for using the framework in this book.
2. PELP faculty members developed this problem-solving model, but similar approaches exist in many continuous improvement processes.
3. Rick DuFour, "Leading Edge: Are You Looking out the Window or in the Mirror?" *Journal of Staff Development* 25, no. 3 (Summer 2004).
4. Stacey Childress, Richard Elmore, and Allen Grossman, "How to Manage Urban Districts," *Harvard Business Review*, November 2006.
5. The "five whys" were developed originally as part of the Toyota Production System and have been adopted and refined as part of the Six Sigma quality improvement process. A similar approach to root cause analysis exists in the Baldrige system and other continuous improvement processes.
6. If your team has significant diagnostic work to perform in this area, consult the "Note on the PELP Coherence Framework" for guiding questions about each piece of your organization; see Stacey Childress, Richard Elmore, Allen Grossman, and Caroline King, "Note on the PELP Coherence Framework," Note PEL-010 (Boston: Harvard Business School, 2007).
7. Adapted from Stacey Childress, "Wireless Generation," Case 9-307-049 (Boston: Harvard Business School, 2006).

Acknowledgments

The candor and insights of the many people in Montgomery County who were interviewed for this project, as well as for the several publications we used as source documents, made this book possible. In part because they were promised anonymity and in part because of sheer numbers, we cannot thank them all by name, but to all the people interviewed—they know who they are—thank you for your courtesy and confidence. Because of their contributions and the work they do every day on behalf of students in Montgomery County, nearly half of the royalties from sales of *Leading for Equity* will support scholarships through the Montgomery County Public Schools Educational Foundation.

Leading for Equity was supported by a generous grant from the Stupski Foundation. The foundation conducted a comprehensive study of Montgomery County Public Schools as part of its effort to help school districts across America learn about successful education reforms. The research team was lead by Dr. Louise Bay Waters and Dr. Stacy L. Scott. Following the study, Dr. Scott joined Montgomery County Public Schools as associate superintendent for the Office of Shared Accountability. Dr. Scott contributed greatly to the content of this book. His insights into and analysis of the MCPS story can be seen throughout the book. We are grateful for his assistance, persistence, and caring spirit throughout the project.

Alicia D. Spain worked tirelessly on an early draft, and her imprint remains throughout the final manuscript. Her good humor, patience, and research and writing standards contributed greatly to the project. Without her efforts, this book would not have seen the light of day.

Karen Mapp and Tonika Cheek Clayton of the Public Education Leadership Project at Harvard University coauthored two seminal cases about race and achievement in MCPS in 2006. Those pieces are the backbone of chapter 6 and influenced other chapters as well. The entire faculty team of PELP, including chairs Allen Grossman and Susan Moore Johnson, were involved in the development of many of the concepts that frame this book's story. Through its founding gift to PELP, the Harvard Business School (HBS) Class of 1963 deserves many thanks for investing in the program that originally connected us to the work in MCPS in 2003. The Division of Research at HBS has also been an unflagging supporter.

As the manuscript developed, Brian Edwards at MCPS made sure that we had access to the people and documents we needed to get the story right, whether at 6:00 a.m. or 11:30 p.m., and he coordinated an internal review team to ensure that we had the facts straight, which was especially important in describing the early years of the strategy. Because of this, Brian and the review team deserve special thanks.

And finally, Geoff Marietta's commitment to the project in its final days made the difference in meeting an aggressive publishing deadline. His understanding of the importance of the MCPS work, his willingness to push everything else aside to focus on the story, and his personal commitment to breaking the link between race, income, and achievement in the United States made him a full partner in *Leading for Equity*. Thank you, Geoff.

Stacey M. Childress
Denis P. Doyle
David A. Thomas
March 2009

About the Authors

Stacey M. Childress is a lecturer at Harvard Business School and a cofounder of the Public Education Leadership Project at Harvard University. She studies the behavior and strategies of leadership teams in urban public school districts, charter schools, and nonprofit enterprises with missions to improve the public system. Childress has authored more than two dozen case studies about large urban districts and entrepreneurial education ventures and is the coauthor of the bestselling *Harvard Business Review* article "How to Manage Urban Districts." She is also a coeditor of the book *Managing School Districts for High Performance: Cases in Public Education Leadership*, Harvard Education Press, November 2007.

Childress teaches in HBS's MBA program, where she has won the Student Association teaching award from the students in her course Entrepreneurship in Education. In 2008, she was an inaugural recipient of the Charles M. Williams award for excellence in teaching, named in honor of one of the school's legendary case method professors.

Denis P. Doyle is cofounder and chief academic officer of SchoolNet. He is a nationally and internationally known education writer and consultant. He began his career as a consultant to the California legislature after earning his AB and MA in political science from the University of California at Berkeley. He later joined the federal government as an assistant director of the U.S. Office of Economic Opportunity, where he developed major education reform projects. He was transferred by executive order to the U.S. Office of Education, where he served as an assistant director of the National Institute of Education. Since that time, Doyle has served in three think tanks—the Brookings Institution, the American Enterprise Institute, and

Hudson Institute—where he has written over two hundred articles for both scholarly and popular publications, ranging from the *Atlantic Monthly* to the *Washington Post*.

An authority on business and education, Doyle is the coauthor of three major education books with CEOs: *Investing in Our Children*, with Procter & Gamble CEO Brad Butler; *Winning the Brain Race*, with Xerox CEO David Kearns; and *Reinventing Education*, with IBM CEO Lou Gerstner.

David A. Thomas is the H. Naylor Fitzhugh Professor of Business Administration at Harvard Business School. He joined the HBS faculty in 1990 and became a tenured professor in 1998. Professor Thomas is a recognized thought leader in the area of strategic human resource management. His research addresses issues related to executive development, cultural diversity in organizations, leadership, and organizational change.

He is coauthor of the bestselling *Harvard Business Review* article "Making Differences Matter: A New Paradigm for Managing Diversity." His book *Breaking Through: The Making of Minority Executives in Corporate America* (with John Gabarro) has met with critical acclaim in reviews by academics and journalists, and is the recipient of the Academy of Management's George R. Terry Book Award for outstanding contribution to the advancement of management knowledge. It explores the career advancement and development of minority executives in large multinational corporations.

Professor Thomas received his BA (1978), MPhil (1984), and PhD (1986) degrees from Yale University. He also holds an MA (1981) in organizational psychology from Columbia University.

Index

accountability, shared, 23, 24, 109, 136–138
Achieve, Inc., 42–43, 44–45
achievement gaps
  about, 2, 112–113
  by geography, 17–18, 19, 27
achievement testing, 102–103
African American students
  achievement gaps, 2, 112–113
  kindergarten reading, 2
  mathematics achievement, 2
algebra, eighth-grade completion, 2, 90, 135, 136
Alvez, Aggie, 65
Anemone, Louis, 105
AP/honors courses enrollment. *See also* Honors/AP Potential Identification Tool (HAPIT)
  about, 2–3, 16, 38, 50–51
  Honors/AP Potential Identification Tool (HAPIT), 107–108, 123, 127, 152
  progress, 125
assessment, student, 45–46

Baldrige Education Criteria for Performance Excellence, 95–96, 162
Barnes, Linna, 22
Bastress, Bob, 85
Bayewitz, Michael, 143
Bedford, Ann, 99–100
Bedford, Steve, 89, 106, 143
Bel Pre Elementary School, 40, 101

blame, culture of, 24
Bowers, Larry, 58, 85
Bratton, William, 105
Broad Acres Elementary School, 87, 116–117, 143
Brook Grove Elementary School, 76
Brown v. Board of Education, 14
business community, as stakeholders, 67–69, 99–101

career lattice, 82–83
Centro Familia, 112
College Board, 42–43, 44–45
college partnerships, 69–70
college-readiness goals, 20, 28, 128, 145
community participation, 24, 25–28
CompStat, 105
Congressional Black Caucus (CBC) Foundation, 68
Congressional Hispanic Caucus (CHC) Institute, 68
Council for Basic Education, 44–45
Courageous Conversations (Singleton), 113, 127
Cox, Sharon, 26
Cullison, Bonnie, 57, 58, 142, 163
"culture of respect" compact, 60–61
culture, school, 138–139
curriculum and instruction
  audit, 41–43
  comprehensive overhaul, 44–45
  kindergarten, 39–41
  standardization, 38–39
Cuttitta, Merle, 57, 59, 142

data-driven decision making
  about, 22, 25, 96–97
  examples, 118
  M-STAT, 105–109
  mCLASS:Reading 3D, 99–101
Deloitte, 68
Department of Education, U.S.,
  145–148
Dewey, John, 3
differentiation, 45, 46–50, 132–134
Diversity Training and Development
  (DTD), 113–115
Duncan, Arne, 146
Duncan, Doug, 62

Early Success Performance Plan, 37
Edwards, Brian, 90
elementary school level
  literacy reform efforts, 36–38
  mathematics curriculum redesign,
  42–43
Emerging Student Leaders program,
  67–68
English for Speakers of Other Languages
  (ESOL), 78
equity practices, 25–26, 35–36, 52–53,
  133, 141–143
Equity Training and Development
  Department, 129
Ervin, Valerie, 112–113
ethnicity. *See* race and ethnicity issues
Everyday Mathematics, 42
expectations, teacher, 80, 111–112,
  138–139

federal government role, 145–148
forecasting, 102–103

Gates, Bill, 147
Gateway to College program, 69–70

Getting to Yes (Fisher and Ury), 57
Gordon, Edmund, 15
The Gordon Report, 15
governance, shared, 23
grading and reporting practices, 16,
  46–50, 139
Graves, Donna, 113, 127

Harcourt, 43
Hermann, Ursula, 119–120
high school level reforms, 2–3, 16, 38,
  50–51
Hispanic students
  achievement gaps, 2, 112–113
  kindergarten reading, 2
  mathematics achievement, 2
Hollingshead, Donna, 109
Honors/AP Potential Identification Tool
  (HAPIT), 107–108, 123, 127, 152
honors courses enrollment. *See* AP/
  honors courses enrollment
human capital, 3–4, 75–76
Hurricane Katrina, 122

Identity, 70
information technology investments, 76,
  97–101
institutional barriers, 94, 121–123, 139,
  140
Instructional Management System, 97–98
Integrated Quality Management System
  (IQMS), 97–98
interest-based bargaining, 57

Kim, Yong Mi, 135
kindergarten
  curriculum development, 39–41
  full-day programs, 37, 41
  reading targets, 102
Kubasik, Jane, 68

Lacey, Frieda, 27, 70, 106, 107, 123, 143
The Larson Report, 16
Latino Civil Rights Task Force of Maryland, 22
Leggett, Isiah, 23
Leleck, Jody, 89, 103–105, 116–117, 143
literacy
  early elementary, 36–38, 52
Lockheed Martin, 90

M-STAT, 105–109, 125, 139, 166–167
magnet schools, 14–15
Maple, Jack, 105
Math MSA Model, 102–103
mathematics program
  curriculum redesign, 42–43
  Mathematics Pathway, 103–105, 135
mCLASS:Reading 3D, 99–101, 139, 162–163
Measures of Academic Progress Reading (MAP-R), 102–103
Merry, Darlene, 51, 113
Minority Leadership Recruitment Committee, 125
minority student achievement
  achievement gaps, 2, 112–113
  The Gordon Report, 15
  Honors/AP Potential Identification Tool (HAPIT), 107–108
  The Larson Report, 16
  Success for Every Student (SES), 15–16
Montgomery College, 69–70
Montgomery County
  demographics, 14–15, 17–18, 19, 35
  Montgomery County Council, 23, 61–64
Montgomery County Association of Administrative and Supervisory Personnel (MCAASP), 56–61, 85–86

Montgomery County Board of Education, 61–64
Montgomery County Business Roundtable for Education (MCBRE), 67–68
Montgomery County Education Association (MCEA), 56–61, 75
Montgomery County Latino Education Coalition, 70
Montgomery County PTA, 22
Montgomery County Public Schools (MCPS). *See also* Weast, Jerry
  achievement gaps, by geography, 17–18, 19, 27
  Baldrige Leadership Team, 95–96
  central administration reorganization, 94–97
  Deputy's Minority Achievement Advisory Committee, 70
  district self-assessment, 95–96
  early successful schools, 116–120
  Equity Training and Development Department, 129
  financial resources, 144–145
  hiring practices, 76–77
  history, 14–17
  information technology and, 97–101
  Minority Leadership Recruitment Committee, 125
  Office of Organizational Development (OOD), 79, 89, 113
  overview, 1–9
  zone divisions, 34–36, 65–66

National Association for the Advancement of Colored People (NAACP), 70
National Labor College, 112
Navarro, Nancy, 112–113, 127, 142
New Hampshire Estates Elementary School, 40
Newman, Rebecca, 57, 58, 85, 142

No Child Left Behind (NCLB) Act, 28,
145–146

Obama, Barack, 3, 146
Office of Organizational Development
(OOD), 79, 89, 113
O'Neill, Patricia, 64
Operational Excellence project (OpEx),
68
*Our Call to Action: Raising the Bar and
Closing the Gap*, 21–28, 64

Parent Advisory Council, 66
parents
communicating with, 115
as stakeholders, 65–66
partnerships, stakeholding, 69–70
Pathway to Success, 48, 103–105
Peer Assistance and Review (PAR)
program, 58, 77, 78, 81,
83–84
Piney Branch Elementary School, 116,
118–119, 143
Porter, John Q., 97
PricewaterhouseCoopers, 68
problem-solving process, for reform
adaptations and modifications of
plan, 168–170
implementation plan, 162–164
problem identification and analysis,
152–157
problem-solving process overview,
150–152
progress assessment, 166–168
strategy design, 159–161
strategy implementation, 164–166
theory of action development,
157–159
professional development (PD)
about, 74–75, 90–91
executive team development, 88–89

Professional Growth System (PGS),
77–78, 81–86
Professional Learning Communities
Institute (PLCI), 87–88
professional learning environments,
77–79
Skillful Teacher courses, 79–80
Professional Growth System (PGS)
about, 58
for administrative staff, 85–86
for instructional staff, 77–78, 81–84
for support staff, 86
Professional Learning Communities
Institute (PLCI), 77, 87–88, 165
professional learning environments,
77–79
PSAT exam participation, 50, 106, 123,
125–126, 135, 151–152
PSAT M-STAT Data Booklet, 125
Public Education Leadership Project
(PELP) at Harvard University. *See
also* problem-solving process, for
reform
Montgomery County Public Schools
involvement, 4, 88–89, 105, 121
problem-solving process overview,
150–152

Quintero, Henry, 22

race and ethnicity issues
discussing, 115, 121–123, 128–129,
140–141
diversity, 125–129
and outcomes link, 122–123, 129,
139–141
Study Circles, 124–125
reading
data tracking, 99–101, 139
kindergarten benchmarks, 2
Research for Better Teaching (RBT), 78, 79

resources
  equitable *vs.* equal distribution of,
    25–26, 35–36, 52–53, 133, 141–143
  focus of, 24
Rolling Terrace Elementary School, 40
Ronald McNair Elementary School, 87
root cause analysis, 154–157
Ruth Rales Comcast Kids Reading
  Network, 70

school culture, 138–139
school reform
  call to action, 143–148
  equal resources *vs.* equal opportunity,
    25–26, 35–36, 52–53, 126
  human capital and, 3–4
  moral imperatives for, 3, 26–27
  overcoming opposition, 51–52
  six assumptions for, 24–25
  six lessons for, 132–143
segregation, 14
Service Employees International Union
  (SEIU) Local 500, 56–61
Seven Keys to College Readiness,
  128
"720" program, 67
Sherwood Elementary school, 96
Shirley, Ed, 57
Silverman, Steve, 62
Simon, Mark, 57
SIMS data system, 96–97
Simulation, Training and Support (STS),
  90
Singleton, Glenn, 113, 127
Skillful Teacher courses, 79–80, 117
stakeholders, 55–56, 71–72
  business community, 67–69, 98–101
  county council, 61–64
  parents, 65–66
  partnerships, 69–70
  school board, 61–64
  unions, 56–61

standards, content area, implementing,
  28–29, 46–50, 93–94, 132–134,
  145–146
  national standards, 145–148
Stetson, Frank, 107
student information systems, 76
student-to-teacher ratios, 37–38
Success for Every Student (SES), 15–16,
  21, 62
Supporting Service Professional Growth
  System (SSPGS), 86

teachers. *See also* professional
    development (PD)
  career lattice, 82–83
  clarifying expectations, 45–46
  and class sizes, 51
  Diversity Training and Development
    (DTD), 113–115
  expectations, 80
  grading and reporting practices,
    46–50
  hiring of, 76–77
  importance, 73
  and new standards, 29
  Peer Assistance and Review (PAR)
    program, 58, 77, 78, 81, 83–84
  Professional Growth System (PGS),
    58, 77–78, 81–84
  professional learning environments,
    77–79
  Skillful Teacher courses, 79–80
technological investment, 97–101, 139
theories of action, 157–159
Tilden Middle School, 96

unions, 56–61, 75, 137–138
UnitedHealthcare, 68
University System of Maryland, 69
Upcounty and Downcounty Latino
  Network, 70

value chain thinking, 134–136
Vance, Paul, 15, 16, 62
Viers Mill Elementary School, 87, 116, 117–118
Virga, Jamie, 87, 89, 118

Waters Landing Elementary School, 96
Wayside Elementary School, 135–136
Weast, Jerry
    about, 4
    arrival, 13, 17–18
    communication style, 27
    early life, 16–17
    executive team development, 88–89
    impact of, 141–142
    recruited to position, 63
    stakeholder relations, 55–70
Westland Middle School, 116, 119–120
Wireless Generation, 98–101, 162
work-readiness goals, 20, 28, 29, 128, 145